Parents as Healers: Bringing the Caregiver into the Healing Process Through Play and Home-Based Strategies

Parents as Healers: Bringing the Caregiver into the Healing Process Through Play and Home-Based Strategies

● ● ●

Anne Marie M Ramos, LCSW, RPT-S

ISBN-13: 9781548299361
ISBN-10: 1548299367

Dedication

● ● ●

**To Risë VanFleet, PhD, RPT-S, CDBC, who taught me
the power of parents to heal their children**

Table of Contents

Introduction ·ix

Chapter 1 Rationale for Using a Parents as Healers Approach· · · · · · · · 1
Chapter 2 Beginnings· 17
Chapter 3 Child Disruptive Disorders: Use of Parent Training· · · · · 30
Chapter 4 Anxiety· 44
Chapter 5 Trauma· 57
Chapter 6 Attention Deficit Hyperactivity Disorder · · · · · · · · · · · · · 65
Chapter 7 Social Skills · 78
Chapter 8 When Things Are Not Working · · · · · · · · · · · · · · · · · · · 86

Appendix · 91
Bibliography· 95

Introduction

● ● ●

I HAD WORKED WITH SARAH and Ed,[1] parents of David, an energetic 8-year-old boy with several challenges including a diagnosis of Attention Deficit Hyperactivity Disorder, (ADHD) for which he received medication, a tendency to suffer from low self-esteem and negative thinking despite the parent's best efforts to support and praise him, frequent oppositional outbursts, inability to make friends, and some additional social issues both with his siblings and among his peers at school. The parents were exhausted by this child who was very different from his three-other mild-mannered siblings. Nevertheless, they were happy to use the "Parents as Healers" approach where they were very active participants in the interventions in the therapy room and at home. Six months later the mother reported that things were considerably better on a consistent basis and they were ready to consider exploring ending sessions. As we discussed the pros and cons of termination, David commented, "I'll be bad again so I can come back!" He clearly was not quite as ready to end as the mother. The mother initially attributed the child's attachment to the therapy and the changes he was able to make to the positive attention he received from me. A few minutes later David, who was playing in the sand tray, came up to his mother and animatedly began talking about something he found in the sand. When he went back to the sandbox I commented, "You know,

---

1 To protect client privacy, case examples throughout this book are composites of several different families with names and circumstances slightly altered. However, they demonstrate families' and children's typical reactions and behaviors as they engage in a *Parents as Healers* approach.

David came to you and not me. I think he's really attached to **your** attention." The mother responded. "I know. You facilitate this." By the end of the session, the three of us were able to come up with an "experiment" to see if David could be sustained by some bonding time with his mother outside of the home for one hour for the next week instead of coming to therapy. We would not make a decision about ending until we evaluated the results of the "experiment."

When I thought about introducing the subject of teaching parents to be healers in the therapy room for this book, I had just experienced this interaction in a therapy session. When Sarah observed, "You facilitate this," I was validated that I communicated how important her role was in the healing process and that she observed that the interventions where she was encouraged to take a leading role, made it happen. In this model, the therapist puts parents in a leadership or co-therapy role as much as possible using an integrative therapy approach, often using play- based interventions. Sometimes, this means meeting with the parent separately to train them in a particular skill or collaborate on next steps. Other times, it may mean having a parent and child play a particular play therapy game designed to accomplish goals with the therapist as coach. On another occasion, the parent may be participating with their child in a multi-sensory psychoeducational presentation regarding their child's challenges. The subsequent chapters will discuss how to do this but this introduction first will address the benefits of having this model as a necessary part of a therapist's "tool kit."

Why use a Parent as Healer Approach?

There is increasing evidence to support the claim that therapy which either includes parent and child together or puts the parent in a pivotal role is more effective than therapy where the child is treated individually. These include mega studies of Filial Therapy, (Cornett & Bratton, 2015; Bratton, Ray, Rhine, & Jones, 2005), where a parent is trained to provide child centered play therapy to his/her child(ren), as well as mega studies on family based treatments from 2001-2013 on a variety of child mental health issues including ADHD, eating disorders, and grief, among others (Carr, 2014). Recent smaller studies about the effectiveness of *Theraplay* where parents learn to provide attachment based play have shown highly promising results (Munns, 2009). One of the most well researched treatments for oppositional defiant and conduct disorders is parent training, where a parent is trained to notice and reward positive behaviors and to either ignore or give consequences for negative behaviors (Eyberg, O'Brian, & Chase, 2006 ; Kazdin & Weisz, 1998). In the child trauma field, popular researcher, Dr. Bruce Perry, creator of the *Neurosequential Model of Therapeutics*, discovered that traumatized children who lack consistent caregivers show arrested brain development (Perry & Hambrick 2008). His findings demonstrate that children who have a consistent supportive caregiver weather trauma better than those who have had unpredictable and unstable relationships (Perry, 2009).

Dr. Perry's research and the studies outlined above suggest that therapy which emphasizes the importance of the parent in healing a child's presenting problems can be more effective than therapy where the child is treated individually or where the parent's involvement is marginalized. Yet today many therapists do divide parents and children (Green, Baggerly, & Myrick, 2015). A typical arrangement I have observed among my colleagues as a clinician and supervisor is to meet with the child for the majority of the session and to "touch base" with the parent for the first or last five or ten minutes without the child. While the therapists are well meaning and trying to include parent input, they are actually marginalizing the parent's involvement while communicating that the more important therapeutic relationship is between themselves and their child. This arrangement may be necessary in some cases, if for example, the bulk of the therapy takes place in a school or residential setting where caregivers cannot be readily available or if severe family estrangement, environmental concerns, or other issues prevent at least temporarily more active caregiver involvement. If a parent is available, why miss an opportunity, for example, for the child to express their feelings directly to the parent through a play therapy game? In this case, the parent is given an opportunity to directly hear from their child and respond in an empathic way.

There is a greater chance that the child will go home to an atmosphere where he is a bit more understood. This is likely to have more impact on the child's healing than knowing that his therapist whom he will not see for another week understands him.

Fortunately, there is a growing interest among practitioners in providing family based treatments. One of the pioneers in developing family based play treatments is Dr. Eliana Gil. For years, she helped children heal through engaging the family in creative play and allowing them to discover their own path to healing as they uncover the metaphors they have created. (Gil, 2015) Gil uses sand tray work, storytelling through puppetry, and visual arts among other techniques to help families creatively express conflicts and feelings which provides a safe supportive atmosphere to facilitate problem solving and change.

Dr. Angela Cavett is another leader in the field of play therapy who supports including the parents in treatment sessions with children. She states "...parents and other caregivers are typically the child's most important advocates. A parent can be a co-therapist in the play therapy process within sessions," (p. 3). Cavett is a proponent of both cognitive behavioral play therapy as well as recognizing the importance of the caregiver. Cavett among others has been practicing and writing about how traditionally individual therapies such as CBT can not only be play based but can also incorporate the caregiver (Green, Baggerly, Myrick, 2015). In the subsequent chapters I will describe how the therapist can engage the parent to be in a therapeutic role both in therapy sessions and at home. In the latter chapters I will describe integrative treatment approaches for a variety of presenting problems using case examples. While I myself often use both Filial Therapy and *Theraplay*®, and highly recommend that every child therapist have a working knowledge of them, I will refer to them in summary form since informative and descriptive books have already been published about these approaches. I hope the reader will note these titles in the bibliography and be inspired to do further reading on these topics. In this book, I will instead focus more in detail on a variety of other approaches including directive play therapy techniques with the family, Cognitive Behavioral Therapy (CBT) and Dialectical and Behavior

Therapy (DBT) oriented treatments, parent training, skills training, child-oriented psychoeducation, and family oriented expressive communication, among others.

CHAPTER 1

Rationale for Using a Parents as Healers Approach

● ● ●

THERAPISTS USING A "PARENTS AS Healer's" (PAH) approach consider the parent or caregiver to be the most important catalyst for change in the child's/adolescent's life. There is much research to support that either training the parent to be the primary "healer" or incorporating them in a dynamic way in the therapy session is effective. Additional evidence supports that it can be even more effective in resolving child/adolescent problems than individual approaches. One of the most studied and efficacious parent-led therapies is Filial Therapy first created by Dr. Bernard Guerney and further developed in conjunction with his wife, Dr. Louise Guerney in the 1960's (Guerney, 1964; Guerney, 2000). In this model, parent participants are trained to provide child-centered play therapy (CCPT) to their children (VanFleet, 2014). CCPT follows the principles of non-directive play developed by Virginia Axline in the 1940's where a child is encouraged to express their feelings and conflicts through creative play with just enough limits to keep themselves, others, and their surroundings safe (Axline, 1947). Filial Therapy provides initial training to the parents which is followed by observed parent-child sessions. The therapist provides supportive feedback to the parents (about 5 or 6 sessions) until they are ready to provide weekly play therapy sessions in the home. The work continues while the therapist provides child guidance and coaches the parent as issues emerge in the play and in other areas of the child's life. The program is ended once goals have been met and a plan to transition the family from Filial Therapy to individualized "special time" with the parents is created. A meta-analysis of play therapy and

Filial Therapy showed that while individual play therapy was effective, Filial Therapy in comparison was more effective by significant numbers (Bratton & Ray, 2005). Since then, studies have continued to support the effectiveness of Filial Therapy to treat a wide range of issues within cross cultural settings (VanFleet, 2014).

An outgrowth of Filial Therapy is Child Parent Relationship Therapy (CPRT) which is a more condensed version of Filial Therapy. In CPRT parents meet in a group setting for 2 hours/week over a 10-week period to learn skills to conduct 7 child centered play sessions with their children on site. (Cornett & Bratton, 2014). Extensive studies on the outcome of this method has shown it to be as effective as the extended Filial Therapy format. (Cornett & Bratton, 2015).

Other effective and widely researched parent-facilitated therapies are treatments for the disruptive or conduct disordered child which includes a strong parent training component. (Eyberg et. al., 2006; Heneggler & Sheidow, 2012; Kazdin, 2006, Michelson et. al., 2013). Many parent training programs share common features such as teaching parents to ignore or punish negative behaviors and praise or reward positive behaviors with consistency. (Eyberg et. al. 2006). One of these programs, Parent-Child Interaction Therapy (PCIT), developed by Shelia Eyberg, is a 20-week manualized approach for children aged 2-7 that have disruptive behavior problems. Through a 'bug in the ear' receiver system, parents are observed from a one-way mirror by the therapists while playing with their child. Through the earpiece, the parents are supportively coached and praised in the moment to have improved child-directed and parent-directed interaction. The goals are ultimately to reduce child behavior problems, improve parenting skills, and enhance parent-child bonding (Urquiza & Timmer, 2012). This program, studied since the 1980's has consistently been found to be highly effective in meeting those goals and there is an effort to increase its application to broader clinical issues (Urquiza & Blacker, 2011). Other programs for disruptive children incorporate the well-researched and highly efficacious Parent Management Training (PMT) which was developed at the Yale Parenting Center and Child conduct Clinic over 20 years ago (Kazdin,1997; Kazdin & Wassel, 2000). This method will be described more in depth in Chapter 3. Most recently the Center has been continuing to use PMT in combination with Problem Solving Skills Training (PSST) with children from pre-school through 14 years of age and their research demonstrates that it continues to provide significant change to severely disturbed disruptive children in inpatient and outpatient settings (Kazdin 2012).

Theraplay® is another effective parent-led approach where parents are trained to have better relationships with their children. The goal of the therapy is to reduce the child's presenting problems through attachment-based play and enhance parent-child bonding. (Boothe & Jernberg, 2010). Jernberg, who developed this model in the 1970's, used attachment theory to form the basis of her method which emphasizes replicating healthy parent-infant bonding. The four principles of the approach are structure, engagement, nurture, and challenge. In the structure domain parents provide safety, organization, and limit setting while in the engagement dimension parents provide opportunities for attunement and shared joy. Parents learn nurturing by responding empathically to the child's needs and in the challenge sphere parents encourage the child to take risks to move him toward mastery (Boothe & Jernberg, 2010). The role of the therapist in *Theraplay*® is to teach parents to promote these principles through the use of interactive and playful games. For example, a structuring activity would be a mirroring game where the child must copy or mirror the hand motions of the parent while an engagement activity would be the "peeka-boo" game (Munns, 2009). Activities are adjusted developmentally according to the age of the child. It is most frequently used for children from 18 months to 12 years yet has been adapted to older populations. While *Theraplay*® does not yet have the advantage of the numerous peer reviewed published research studies as the above approaches, there is a growing body of national and international research that supports the efficacy of this approach (Munns, E. & Munns, C., 2015; Munns, E., 2009; Weir et. al. 2013).

There is a significant body of research in the field of family therapy that demonstrates the effectiveness of involving the family for child related problems. (Carr, 2014). These therapies can include those mentioned above such as PCIT and parent training but can also include other systemic therapies such as multi-systemic therapy (MST) where families receive intensive treatment often in the home or community. In a meta-analysis of family therapy, Carr (2014) has provided evidence to support the effectiveness of family therapy to treat a wide range of child related problems. These include sleep, feeding, attachment, abuse, conduct, ADHD, anxiety, school refusal, depression, and eating disorders. Carr also makes the point that previous studies done by Crane & Christenson indicated that family therapy reduces health service usage and is associated with greater benefits than individual therapy. Crane & Christenson (2012) studied data from the Kansas Medicaid system and found that while patients' health improved with individual therapy, there was even greater improvement with marital and family therapy and was more cost effective. Further research from other studies indicated that family therapy was more effective than individual work for treating anorexia nervosa and runaway adolescents (Guo & Slesnick, 2013; Robin et. al., 1999). Clearly research in the field of family therapy indicates the efficacy of involving the caregiver in the treatment of child/adolescents and it also indicates areas where it has demonstrated greater benefits over individual approaches.

A PAH approach is consistent with the findings of Dr. Bruce Perry, prominent researcher and speaker on trauma-informed therapy and co-author of *The Boy Who Was Raised as a Dog.* Dr. Perry found that relationship stability and consistency in a child's life was crucial to his ability to effectively heal from trauma. (Perry 2009). While more will be discussed in a subsequent chapter about the specific nature of his research, the point made here is that because a PAH approach with traumatized children includes and supports the caregiver and caregiver/child relationship as a priority, it is consistent with the aspect of trauma informed research that finds children require support and predictability from caregivers to survive trauma.

Since the research points to the efficacy of including the caregiver in the treatment process, one might ask why there is a need for a PAH approach when so many "tried and true" methods already exist? First, the methods described above point to specific therapies for often a specific range of presenting problems. A PAH approach is, in comparison, initially, a framework which helps therapists and families with beginnings and formulating a collaborative relationship where the caregiver is encouraged to be a dynamic part of developing hypotheses and treatment planning and to be active in the upcoming interventions with the child. It sets the stage where the family and therapist can then choose a parent-led manualized evidence based intervention, an adapted one, or an integrated approach with an active role for the caregiver.

Manualized evidence based treatment plans are those that come with an instruction manual which often defines what to do in each session and have been proven through studies to be effective. Therapists need to be trained in the method and need to have access to the manual for the therapy to be implemented correctly. Some manualized programs have already been mentioned above such as PMT, PCIT, and CPRT. Manualized programs have varying degrees of flexibility built in depending on the curriculum. Other evidence based methods such as cognitive behavioral therapy may reflect a broader set of interventions and may not have a definitive manual. While it can be ideal when a child's circumstances and presenting issues can "match" an evidence based method, at times, the intervention may simply not be practical or feasible in a particular clinic setting. Furthermore, it may not be an appropriate treatment plan for a child with the complexity of internal, family, and environmental issues facing him or her. Studies of evidence based programs are often done in researcher controlled setting in specified conditions, for example in university or hospital settings (Sprenkle 2012). Clients with co-morbid conditions or more severe problems may be excluded, for example. These conditions may not reflect the majority of the types of clients assigned to a clinician's typical caseload. As a result, there can often be a disconnect between an evidence based intervention and one that is useable for the clinician (Kazdin, 2008). Sprenkle (2012), in a meta-analysis for effective family interventions further observed that many top-rated models did not "transport" or get used by clinics. He stated: "In the absence of extensive, truly real-world "transported" research, it is by no means clear whether even the most impressive programs whose research support appears in the leadings journals, (a) will work as well in practice settings and/or (b) will be considered practical/feasible enough by clinicians or clinical organizations to implement them, and/or (c) will be considered interesting or engaging enough by clinicians so that they will use the models if they are not receiving funding or "forced" by external incentives to do so." (p. 10). An example of the difficulty in applying evidence based treatment occurred in a case I had consulted on just recently: A young mother with 6 children was being provided treatment for herself and her family in a program that services families exposed to domestic violence. The mother, diagnosed and treated for mental illness, was seen as overly harsh in her manner and having difficulty connecting emotionally with her children yet highly motivated for help. The therapist and I felt she and the children could benefit from either Filial Therapy, PCIT or *Theraplay*® but the parent needed to bring all 6 children with her to every appointment during the time the grant funded transportation arranged to pick her up. Even if the agency could find volunteers, she would need to brings at least 3 young children with her in the therapy room at all times. The logistics alone made it impossible to do any of the programs named above without major modification since they require working one on one with a parent and child. There was additional concern that the children who were not being worked with and also needed to feel a sense of attachment would feel even more excluded if they were always "left" with volunteers while attending our program. We concluded that a better plan would be to create an adapted program, one which was based on the ideas of Filial Therapy, *Theraplay*®, and parent training, with added relaxation training for the mother. The ideas would have to work while three or more young children were present at a time taking turns. Activities would incorporate "family yoga," "in-vivo" parental coaching and support, and the encouragement of nurturing play oriented group games. The clinician is constantly facing dilemmas such as the one above where the evidence based approach is simply not feasible for a particular client or doable in the clinic setting and needs to be adapted to the client's situation. The PAH therapist can help collaborate with the parent and child(ren), finding creative ways of adapting approaches to meet needs.

Another reason for the need for a PAH approach is to help facilitate integrated treatment plans. Integrated approaches combine several different therapeutic approaches to meet the often multi-dimensional, co-morbid aspects of the child's difficulty (Peabody & Schaefer, 2016). They are widely regarded in the field of child therapy as effective ways to treat the complex issues facing children and adolescents (Zequaj, 2015; Green & Myrick, 2014; Schaefer & Drewes, 2014). It is important to note that integrative treatment is not only a highly-regarded way of working with complex issues, but in this information age, parents, adolescents, and sometimes children ask for specific interventions that they either read about on the internet, saw on YouTube, or were recommended to them by their child's psychiatrist, educational psychologist. or pediatrician. Sometimes clients have even started using some therapeutic techniques through a smart phone app they are finding helpful that they would like the therapist to help them continue with. It is entirely possible that we may not be starting with a "blank slate," and the need for collaborating effective integrative approaches is key. For example: A parent who came to a clinic reported their 8-year-old male child was challenged by impulsivity, social skills deficits, low self-esteem, and anxiety. The parent was most concerned about the anxiety symptoms and consulted with a psychiatrist who did not prescribe medication but wanted the child to try psychotherapy first and recommended cognitive behavioral therapy (CBT). The parent came to the clinic requesting a therapist who was knowledgeable about CBT approaches. (There will be more about CBT in Chapter 4). At intake, the assigned clinician made note of the child's anxiety, yet also noticed that the parents tended to give in to the child's impulsive tendencies and then became overly punitive when he did something outrageous. The therapist felt there was a need for the parents to put some structure in the home with positive reinforcement and consequence so that the child could begin practicing impulse control. She suspected that the structure might help to reduce the child's anxiety by providing external control for impulsive behavior. With a plan in place, the therapist thought she could also provide CBT for both the anxiety and low self-esteem. The CBT sessions, provided with play-based approaches, could provide a space where the parents have time to focus on their son and praise him for his accomplishments, reinforcing bonding, which may also help bolster his self -esteem. Social skills training could occur at a later date. If the parent agreed with this plan, the clinician would have incorporated CBT, parent training, parent/child bonding, and social skills training in one treatment plan. The PAH approach guides the caregiver as integrative methods are woven into the child's treatment in a collaborative way. The caregiver in turn helps to personalize the method to their child and continues the therapy using home based strategies to allow integrative approaches to be more successful.

Finally, as with other parent led and parent facilitated therapies, in a PAH approach parents/caregivers can see, experience and hear, their children's feelings, emotions, in "real time," rather than hearing it "second hand" from the therapist. This has greater impact and enables them to have a greater degree of understanding. In addition, the therapist can role model therapeutic responses which the parent may find helpful as they navigate through the child's challenges. The caregiver, in turn, in a healing role, will learn skills throughout the therapy that they will have over the life of the child which can reduce the need for services in the future. Through the collaboration, the therapist can better and more immediately learn from the parent and child what is working and what is not, making treatment more effective. The therapist can also learn from the caregiver about the child's triggers and learn how he copes on a weekly basis.

The caregiver is in a position to provide help during the week when the child is not in therapy and can continue the therapeutic work which was "jump started" during the treatment session.

Frequently the child does not "act up" or get triggered during their Wednesday 4:15 to 5:00 therapy appointment but rather at bedtime, just before school, at homework time, fighting with siblings, etc. This approach strengthens parents who are in essence "first responders" to their children's pain.

SUMMARY
The PAH approach is a spring board to begin a therapeutic collaborative approach between therapist and caregiver where the caregiver is

encouraged to take an active role in the healing process. Interventions chosen could be manualized, evidence-based approaches, adapted ones, or integrated approaches which may combine one of the first two with other methods to meet the complex needs of the child or adolescent. Whenever possible, the caregiver is encouraged to take an active role in the treatment as much research indicates that it has not only proven to be effective for child/adolescent problems but it has often proven to be more effective than individual approaches. This is not to suggest that "one size fits all" as an individual approach may indeed work better for a particular child/adolescent within a particular family environment. However, it does suggest that involving the caregiver in the ways mentioned above and suggested throughout this book should be explored before being completely ruled out. To introduce the PAH approach in hopefully an engaging way for the Reader, I will describe clinicians' resistance (for good reasons!) for involving the caregiver in a more active role in treatment and demonstrate how this method can enhance the work they are doing with their clients if implemented in a creative and sensitive way.

Too Needy

Brenda, an employee starting her second year of employment after graduating a year and a half ago stated, "I tried a few times having the mother in the room for a joint session but she talks too much about her own issues in front of the child and he gets no attention and feels uncomfortable. I have stopped trying."

When I hear statements like this either in a supervisory or consultant role I ask, "Did you prepare the parent beforehand regarding what you were going to do in the session and the rationale for it?" "If so, did she agree?" "Were your materials prepared for your intervention and did you provide structure?" "If all this was done and the mother still drifted to inappropriate conversations did you, with compassion redirect her or ask her to continue the conversation either later in the session without the child present or on another day?" "Did you assess prior to the intervention how many minutes the parent would be able to tolerate, with support, a child oriented intervention?"

Typically, I have found that when a parent does not "behave" in the therapeutic manner the therapist wishes, the therapist has not collaborated with the parent regarding the intervention and explained their role and sometimes goals have not been clarified. The therapist has not structured the intervention. For example, she has not developed a plan and does not have games or art materials conveniently located. The parent is often unaware of the therapist's expectations and does what comes naturally. Brenda's natural politeness simply reinforced the parent's overly talkative and needy behavior and it is likely that this behavior would not occur if Brenda prepared the parent. Sometimes, however, a parent requires that some of her needs be met in order for her to be present for her child. In a PAH approach, the therapist has a great deal of flexibility on whom to see when. One option I have observed that has often worked successfully with this dynamic is to divide the session with the first part being for the parent and child which is centered on the child and the second part, just for the parent individually. An alternative to this is to periodically provide an individual session to the parent for support, child guidance, or simply to "regroup." Of course, highly stressed parents may need additional services such as case management, psychiatric follow up, individual or marital therapy, etc.

Too Critical

Sam, a veteran therapist of 10 years can successfully engage adolescent boys in individual treatment and is proud of his accomplishments. He tried a parent/child session and stated: "The mother was highly critical of her son in session and her son became stubbornly silent. It was difficult to redirect the parent especially when the son was being quiet. I cannot expose the son to such a situation ever again!

The obvious challenge to this plan is the fact that the child is exposed to his mother's anger on a daily basis as the mother is exposed to the child's withdrawal and provocative behavior. The therapist's desire to "protect" the child with 45 minutes of "sanctuary" in the individual session is not likely to be sufficient to prepare him for the "boxing ring" which is the parent-child relationship.

A PAH approach is best presented in the first session where the therapist can present himself as the family worker. This allows more flexibility of roles and will be described more in depth in the next chapter. If the therapist has already defined himself as the child's individual worker and provides a period of individual sessions where the parent's involvement is marginalized, it may be difficult to switch to parent-child sessions or to add parent management training if there is a difficult first session. The child may say, "I don't want my parent to come into MY session and you can't meet with my parent!" The therapist has unwittingly communicated that the child somehow "owns" the time and space of the therapy appointment and to a large extent is in charge. The therapist may be stuck between wanting to honor an implicit contract between himself and the child and giving the child the opportunity to be exposed to an intervention that could be more effective toward healing the problem the child came in with.

There are ways of structuring a first session so that both parent and child would want to repeat the experience. In Sam's case, he could have begun the session by asking the mother, "Tell me five things about your son that make you proud and then name two challenges." Sam could have prepared the mother in advance by telling her he was going to be asking her these questions. He could also mention that at the first session he would not try to solve the problems but to simply identify some of them and pave the way for a second session. He could let the mother know that he would follow up the discussion with a structured family communication activity to help him get to know both of them and their family in a relaxed and playful way. Games like *Family Happenings* [2], *Warm-up Ball* and the *Ungame Teen's Version* are all appropriate for teens and parents. Once Sam outlined his plan to the mother he could ask for her feedback. It is likely that she would either agree or would suggest a few modifications that Sam could incorporate. With the mother's collaboration, Sam is much less likely to have the scenario described above, but even if the mother began to be critical, the built-in structure of the session and the

---

2 Information regarding accessing these games can be found in the appendix.

preparation regarding expectations would make it difficult for the mother to incessantly complain and easier for Sam to redirect her.

Sam does not need to give up on family work even if his first session is disappointing and even if the adolescent refuses to be seen with his mother in the future as a result. Sam can use his creativity. For example, he can acknowledge his mistake in not planning a better appointment and ask his client to give it another 10-minute try, just to do an activity. Sam can then do the planning described above if the client agrees. Another idea is for Sam to tell his client that he periodically must meet with the mother anyway as the agency requires that all parents have at least 2 parent training sessions during the course of treatment. Sam may be able to engage the adolescent in what he thinks his parent needs the most help in for the training session.

No Knowledge

Michael is an experienced therapist with advanced training in several areas including Obsessive-Compulsive Disorder (OCD) and Cognitive Behavioral Therapy (CBT). He uses an effective manualized treatment method for OCD which he has expertly adapted for children and adolescents. He likes to do his program for the clients he works with individually and then discusses with the parents afterward the points of the program and what they should do. Michael wonders, "Why have parents in the room when I am doing my program? It will be awkward and they will have too many questions. They will just be watching me and the child and both of us will feel self-conscious!"

In subsequent chapters, readers will learn how parents with little or no knowledge of their child's mental health or developmental challenges can be an asset in the session. They can be a dynamic part of a psycho-education session, a supportive "audience," and an active listener. They can be instructed to read a special page from a workbook and to do an activity with their child on a coping skill among other things. Soon they will be giving the therapist ideas about what will work for their child in treatment sessions. While therapists have knowledge about the nature of an illness and effective treatments, parents have a wealth of knowledge from observing their child hours per day on a daily basis. Michael will learn that giving the parents a more prominent role in the healing process by allowing them to be present and active in the session and collaborating with them will make his manualized treatments more dynamic and effective.

KIDS CLAM UP

Margaret, a play therapist for 15 years loves to do individual play therapy with children who respond well to her. She has separate sessions with the parents with whom she provides parent training but gets frustrated because the parents do not seem to understand the children in the way she does. Because her clients open up to her through play she feels she sees a window into their inner world which either gets lost in translation through the ethical bounds of confidentiality or through explaining what happened in the past tense and in the third person. For example, Margaret observed 7-year-old Jessica comment with a very sad expression, "Mommy has no time to play." Jessica's play often portrays a baby bunny alone in the forest while the animal family does activities, ignoring the baby bunny. Margaret expressed to the family her concerns that one of Jessica's issues is her loneliness in the busyness of the family and strongly urged them to spend at least 15 minutes of alone time with her per day. While they agreed to do this in the office, when she catches up with them the next week, they say that something disrupted their week like visiting relatives, a power outage, car issues, etc. and they did not yet get to do it. They then go on to recount their frustration with their daughter's misbehavior.

Margaret decided to switch methods and bring the parents in for a session hoping Jessica would open up to them in the way she open up to her. After the session, Margaret commented, "My client clammed up when her parents were in the room. I can do so much better therapy if the parent is away."

The challenge to this statement is that by proceeding with individual therapy, Margaret may certainly win the battle but not the war. Jessica may feel supported and validated by her therapist but is misunderstood by the most important people in her life. In a PAH approach, the relationship between parent and child and especially the ability of the child to communicate thoughts and feelings to their parent would take priority, especially in this case, over the therapist/child relationship. If the child was opening up more to the therapist than the parent, in this approach, the therapist would see things as off balance and would work toward changing this pattern. Margaret's dilemma would not have occurred if she identified herself as the family worker and started to include the parents in the therapy right away. As with the other case examples, switching to a PAH approach may be more challenging if one started out with an individual therapy approach but if it is done in a positive and sensitive way it can be successful.

An option for Margaret would be to introduce the concept of Filial Therapy to the parents. Filial Therapy, as described above could help the parents slow down and connect with their child and enable Jessica to continue to benefit from CCPT. If Filial Therapy was not feasible or agreed to, an alternative would be to design a creative art activity or other bonding activity for part of the session while keeping the remainder of the session the same. The client might not be ready to "give up" the individual time with her therapist. As time went on the family could reevaluate and see if the child is ready for longer family sessions. Initial creative art activities could include working as a family to create a fantasy island or a zoo. Markers, cut-outs that can be decorated and pasted on, stickers, paint, and other art materials can be provided. A more active child may enjoy the *I am Proud Ball* game or the Feelings Dart Gun Game, where a child shoots a dart gun with a rubber tip at a feelings poster. The child talks about a time he had a feeling where the dart gun lands. The child can alternate turns with his parent. A third option is for the family to choose puppets and create a puppet show. Dr. Eliana Gil gives instructions that participants are to work as a family, create a show with a beginning, middle and end, and enact the show, not narrate it. (Gil, 2015). As the metaphor evolves from the story in subsequent sessions there is opportunity for the family to creatively process it and what it means for them. The metaphoric family play therapy described by Gil can be a powerful way for families to connect, express feelings, and solve interpersonal family dilemmas in a creative and non-threatening way.

Too Dysfunctional!

Kiana, a clinical social worker with five years post graduate experience is working with 8-year-old Hillary whose mother is being seen by another worker in the same mental health facility. Hillary's mother Susan, is a single parent, diagnosed with bipolar disorder and borderline personality disorder. She treats Hillary as a confidant, often seeking her advice on adult subjects and at other times can explode at her for normal childhood requests and behavior. Hillary reacts to this behavior by being overly reactive herself and tends to be bossy with her peers. Teachers are worried about her low frustration tolerance and her inability to make friends. Kiana feels that her weekly appointments and her relationship are the only normalizing influence in the child's life. Parenting guidance done by the mother's therapist seems to have little impact. When the suggestion was made to add some parent bonding sessions to the work, Kiana responded, "This parent is too dysfunctional to have therapy with her child."

Kiana is concerned that the parent is so dysfunctional she will fail at any bonding sessions making the child feel even more adrift and unanchored. She is also concerned that the bonding sessions will dilute the limited therapeutic time she has with Hillary which she feels is vital to the child's emotional wellbeing. While Kiana's reasoning is sound, a PAH approach envisions the problem a bit differently. Since this approach puts a high priority on the parent-child relationship there would be a constant focus on how to improve filial bonding regardless of parental pathology. Adding an extra family session if feasible may satisfy the therapist's and child's reluctance to end individual sessions while improving the child-caregiver relationship. Should this not be feasible, a successful bonding session could be facilitated in 15 minutes followed by a 30-35-minute individual session. This could pave the way to beginning to teach the mother experientially how to more successfully care for her child.

An especially successful treatment for this parent and child could be *Theraplay®* described above where a parent is trained to do simple fun bonding activities with her child once different dimensions of her parenting abilities are evaluated. Filial therapy would also be an option. Both Filial therapy and Theraplay have proven to be effective with highly dysfunctional parents, possibly because they are activity based and there is a great deal of positive support built in from the therapist for the parent. If neither of these methods are feasible, the therapist could use her own creativity. For example, a parent and child could work side by side and design their own T shirts using fabric paint. The activity of sitting together may be all that the parent and child can productively do at first. If they are ready, each of them can add something to the other's T shirt with the owner's permission. This symbolic bonding in an artistic expression can open the door to more effective bonding, communication, and parenting.

CONCLUSION

A PAH approach can most easily be implemented if it is introduced in the assessment phase, however it is possible to switch to this method if it is done with creativity and planning. The success of this method depends on several factors including presenting oneself as the family worker, gaining consensus with the family on goals and interventions, keeping the care-givers engaged and involved and keeping the focus on the power of the parents to heal.

CHAPTER 2

Beginnings

● ● ●

FEW COULD ARGUE WITH THE importance of including the caregiver in the development of the assessment of the child. The highly-regarded Child Behavior Checklist, a measure often used for pre- and post-testing in research and clinic setting to assess children's progress is one that is filled out by parents (Auchenbach, 1991; Ivana et. al. 2001). Caspe et. al. (2013) observed, "A child's first assessors are her family. Is she hungry? Does her diaper need to be changed? How is she growing?" In a PAH approach parents' observations as well as hypotheses about why their child is symptomatic is important. Questions such as, "Do you have any "theory" as to why your child is acting this way?" can elicit important information about the direction of treatment. A child also has his or her own ideas about their symptoms. For example, the statement, "If my baby brother wouldn't breathe so loud I wouldn't need to hit him," is as important for the clinician to know as, "I miss my Mommy too much when I go to school so I cry and go to the nurse."

ASSESSMENT TOOLS

In this age of evidence based research, there is a focus on assessment tools and pre-and post-testing to prove effectiveness of treatment. Agencies and practitioners are now pressured like those in the public-school system, to prove their effectiveness by hoping participants will show improvement on various pencil and paper or computer tests. These tests are great for the computer and provide easy to read graphs but I question their absolute reliability. Having done these for many years myself I see how limited they are in providing assessment information or determining how much a client has improved. I have often observed a client fill out a questionnaire or checklist where the child will score as having no problems, only to speak verbally to the caregiver, client, siblings, and school and find a deeper and richer profile of a symptomatic child, troubled family, and stressful environment. Conversely, I have seen major improvement verbally reported by the parent and client, himself and observed by the therapist and teacher yet surprisingly the post-testing questionnaire has not captured this change. Howarth et. al. (2015) did research on children exposed to domestic violence and found that children and their families measured success in treatment through a rich and wide range of factors such as a "sense of empowerment," the "ability to cope with challenge," and improved quality in the relationship between parent and child. It is difficult to envision how behavioral questionnaires focusing on symptoms would accurately capture these accomplishments. A practitioner should keep in mind that the questionnaire or other paper/pencil assessment tools is only one measure of the child or family system, to be taken in combination with other information such as the child's and parent's verbal reports, observations, and school and community reports for accurate evaluations.

INTAKE APPOINTMENTS

There are a myriad of ways to do an effective assessment in a PAH Approach. One of the most important principles in the beginning as mentioned above is to present oneself as the family worker or more specifically as a facilitator to help the family, especially the caregiver, heal their child. This concept can be communicated explicitly in words or can simply be communicated by the actions and activities of the therapist.

My favorite way to do an assessment is to ask for the child and caregivers to be present for the first session. I usually do not initially ask for the siblings unless they are included in the presenting problem. Over the phone, I get a thumbnail sketch of the problem and tell the parents how

I will conduct the interview so they can be prepared. The following is a typical script:

1. *"I will begin the session by getting to know your child(ren) and chit chat with them so I can get to know their strengths and they can get to know me.*
2. *I will then ask them if they know why they are here. If they shrug or cannot tell me I will ask you to explain to them some of your concerns.*
3. *Next, we will talk a bit about the problem and any background information and family history you feel comfortable sharing with your child and me.*
4. *Toward the end, I will ask your child to wait in the waiting room while you have a chance to tell me anything you do not feel comfortable speaking about in front of your child.³ "*

Once the outline of the session is given, parents have a chance to comment about how they think it will work or will not work and the therapist can adjust as needed, e.g., a parent might say, "My child will be too scared to leave the room," or "My child will not say a word," or "My child thinks he/she has no problems." Perhaps the child will need a longer "warm up" period or a game before discussing the problem or the parent needs to be empowered to say what their concern is regardless of the child's defiant reaction, knowing that the therapist can handle it in an effective and empathic way.

When the therapist meets with the family for the first time it is important to keep to the agreed upon structure unless something highly unexpected happens, e.g., the child refuses to get out of the car, requiring the therapist and family to change strategies. If there is a strategy change, it is best to include the parents in the decision-making process. In the above

---

3 Frequently a child may be too young or too nervous to go into the waiting room alone. In that case I keep the child in the room with the parents and play a family feelings or communication game and meet with the parents separately the next week or speak with them over the phone.

example the therapist might say, "Your child will not get out of the car. What if I go out to the car and introduce myself?"

Family Play Sessions

Another way to assess family function and strengths are through family play sessions which are well researched evidenced based ways of gathering data the therapist would not receive in structured interviews or questionnaires. (Koehler, Wilson, Baggerly, 2015) They give the therapist the opportunity to observe family interactions in a fun and low pressure setting.

There are a variety of ways to conduct a family play session for assessment and I will outline just a few of them here. Van Fleet (2014) describes one method where the therapist explains to the parent prior to the session that she will be watching the family play together to observe how the identified child interacts with family members for 20-30 minutes from either a one-way mirror, another room with a video camera, or from a corner of a room. The therapist will then ask the family how typical their interactions resemble those at home.

Another variation to the family play assessment is to ask family members to rally around a particular task, for example, to work as a family to create a scene in the sand or to create a fantasy island, zoo, or aquarium with markers, cut outs, stickers and other art materials on a big piece of mural paper or poster board. The therapist can then ask each family member what they contributed to the project and how typical or atypical their interactions were during this activity compared to how they relate at home. Atypical reactions can be just as illuminating as typical reactions because family members can speculate why this happened. For example, a normally well behaved child might have acted out because she did not want to be "dragged" to the session that day. I once observed a large family of parents and five children in a play session for assessment. At the conclusion of the session. I asked, "Was this typical behavior for your children?" The parents responded, "Absolutely not. They were so well behaved here; we never saw anything like it!"

A side benefit of a family play session early in the treatment period is to help solidify the therapist's role as family worker. This role is key to being flexible within the family system which can be beneficial as the treatment period goes on. For example, a frequent phenomenon I have observed is the tendency for a sibling to either "start" acting up or finally get noticed when the presenting problems of the identified patient (I.P) are well on their way to becoming resolved. If the therapist is seen as the family worker, the I.P. rarely has a problem allowing the therapist to address the issues of the siblings and more typically becomes proactive, asking therapists to help other family members, including parents!

GOAL SETTING

Once a therapist has enough information to begin developing, along with the caregiver and child(ren), a working definition of the problem(s) and a couple of hypotheses regarding why it occurred, goals and interventions can be established. These may remain static or may change throughout the treatment period but the goals and interventions established help anchor the family to the work and enable the therapist to function as a co-therapist or collaborator with the parent. There is considerable research to support the efficacy of working collaboratively on goals and interventions with clients. In a meta-analysis, which studied client's preferences for therapy, it was found that improved outcomes and fewer dropouts were achieved when clients choices were accommodated. These included type of treatment, therapist, or the role of the therapist (Tompkins et. al., 2013; Swift, 2009). It is unclear whether client preferences are always considered. Lewin et. al. (2014) found that a majority of parents whose children suffered from Obsessive Compulsive Disorder (OCD) preferred exposure and response prevention therapy (ERP) over medication. Their research indicates that despite this, prescription rates for youth are rising. They state, "It is critical that providers assess patient attitudes toward treatment and preferences where there are choices available." The American Psychological Association (APA) put out a statement regarding Evidence-Based Practice in Psychology (EBPP) at the APA Presidential Task Force in 2006 which states: "EBPP is the integration of the best available research with clinical expertise in the context of patient characteristics, culture, and preferences (APA 2006).

The PAH therapist finds that collaborating with the child and family on goals and interventions can not only make the work more effective but if done creatively can be fun. Dr. Angela Cavett in *Structured Play Based Interventions* (2009) describes a child friendly intervention where she tells a story about how therapy is "like a caterpillar making a cocoon and changing into a butterfly" (p. 43). She explains that therapy helps to change behaviors and has children and parents use art materials to create a caterpillar, cocoon, and butterfly. She then has the children mount their creations on construction paper. After processing with the family, the child writes the problem, such as not listening to teachers or parents under the caterpillar. Under the cocoon, the child writes the interventions or the things to learn, e.g. learn how to calm down, learn how to solve problems that make me angry without getting in trouble, etc. The final step is where the child writes the changes expected under the butterfly, e.g., I will listen to my teachers, I will get better grades, etc. Clinicians can use their own creativity based on the child or adolescent's interest and developmental level to develop treatment plans. One activity I enjoy doing with active and impulsive or reactive children is to have them or their parent write a sign saying what the goal behavior they would like to strive for, e.g., *listen better.* I then have them tape it to the wall. Next, I have their parents trace their feet on paper with or without their shoes on and cut out three or four molds of their feet. On each cut out I write the steps we discussed we would need to take to get to the goal, e.g., *earn points* (in a behavior modification plan at home), *learn self- talk cool down strategies, tell parents and me when things are not fair, learn great problem-solving skills.* We then tape the cut outs on the floor making giant steps and challenge the child to step on the "feet" and touch the sign. This activity gives the child a sense of the process of therapy and a sense of mastery and hope even if it turns out that the goals or interventions become modified or changed along the way.

CHALLENGES IN DEVELOPING GOALS WITH CHILDREN AND PARENTS
CHALLENGE #1:

The therapist suspects that the way the parent and child are defining the problem is actually an adaptation to a much larger issue. For example, the presenting problem for 7-year-old Jose was oppositional and aggressive behavior to his mother for the past few months which coincided with his move from the domestic violence shelter to permanent housing. The therapist hypothesized that due to the timing of the behavior, the child may be having some adjustment issues to the new situation and possibly some unresolved trauma is finally being processed. She recommended that the problem initially be defined as an adjustment issue and that mother and son do some family processing sessions about the recent changes and to explore the family's traumatic past.

CHALLENGE #2

A child may deny having a very obvious problem or will constantly blame others, never taking responsibility. He may make statements like:

"All the other kids in class do the same thing as me but I am the only one who gets suspended."

"The girls are all mean and they don't like me," (despite reports that the child is bossy and critical of her peers.)

"I HAVE to beat up my little brother all the time because my mother just gives him time out and he will never learn not to touch my *Legos*!"

What usually works for me is to reframe the problem in words the child may buy into even if I may have to minimize the problem a bit, e.g.,

"Do you wish you weren't so bothered by your brother so you could maybe get in trouble less often?"

"Do you wish that kids would like you more?" If so, I think we can try some new skills that may work!"

"I know you think the teachers are against you and I am going to ask them to do some things we discussed that may make school better for you but in order to do that we need to let them know you are practicing some skills that will keep you from being suspended. Is that a deal?"

Sometimes reframing does not work and the agreement on goals is with the parent only while the child is along for the ride. If, however, the therapy has a strong parent training component and interventions remain fun for the child, it is likely the child will go along with the program and will eventually start talking about a goal or change he would like to make.

CHALLENGE #4

Sometimes it is not useful for goals to be too specific. For example, a family who has suffered from years of domestic violence and is finally in a shelter may just want to simply learn to adjust to their new reality and begin to talk about what they experienced in order to get through each day. The same idea applies to a family that is recently grieving a loss and the challenges of bereavement may be ever changing. In these types of situations, flexible weekly goals depending on their experiences and struggles may be more effective.

CHALLENGE #5

Parenting goals can be more effective when not always shared with the child or adolescent. For example, a parent may want to develop either better limit setting or more empathy for their child. If the child has been made a part of this discussion a child may experience a parent's changes as not genuine. "You are just saying that because the therapist told you to," a child may retort when he observes the parent praising him. Additionally, other interpersonal goals may need to be worked on without the child present in order for the work to proceed. For example, in order for the parent to begin to develop patience, he may need a place to say, "Sometimes, I hate my child and then I feel guilty, and then I feel angry at my child for making me feel guilty so I snap at her." The therapist has an opportunity to validate the parent's feelings and to help the parent figure out ways to break the pattern.

CHALLENGE #6

A child may be embarrassed to have an issue discussed. For example, he may be ashamed about being suspended from school or having no friends, or feel humiliated about having a toileting issue. A therapist, in wanting to spare the child embarrassment, may believe that never bringing up the issue will be helpful to the child, making him feel more at ease. This will certainly solve one problem but might create several larger ones including that the therapist's hands will be tied to an extent and that another type of anxiety, the elephant in the room that cannot be discussed, will be present. While this is certainly a judgement call on the part of the therapist, generally I find that if a conversation with the child is balanced with a strong look at his strengths and if problem areas are universalized, e.g., "Lots of kids your age struggle with toileting, that's why they come to see me!" embarrassment can be minimized and the work can proceed.

CHALLENGE #7

I recently consulted with a colleague who asked about extreme resistance at the first session. For example, the child or adolescent does not want to be there and refuses to talk, retreating into angry sullen silence. In a PAH approach this rarely happens because the parents are part of the planning of the first appointment however it can happen either to the parent's surprise or the parents suspect it will happen and can pre-plan. These are some tools and techniques I have used effectively to engage a resistant child at the intake stage.

1. I do not show initially that I am put off by stand offish body language or behavior but that I am excited to meet the child and I try to engage him in conversation.
2. If this does not work, I guess what he might be feeling. "I'm guessing you did not want to come here today." Or "I bet you wish this lady would just leave you alone."
3. If I get some kind of acknowledgement, I would see if he could start to talk to me about not wanting to come or what he would rather have been doing, etc.

4. If this still does not work, I look to the parents to help and we talk about what we think the child may be feeling, inviting the child to comment.

5. In many cases this is enough to begin the intake. The child, even if he is not speaking, is relaxed enough to hear, "I am going to ask your parents some of the things they are proud of about you and some of the things they are concerned about and if there is anything they say you disagree with you can let me know." The child usually starts joining in.

6. Sometimes a truly resistant child does not "allow" their parents to say a word. In this case, I tell the parents that today we will just work on engagement. The parents and I will do an activity that the child is periodically invited to join in on. We may make a mural with paint, markers, and stickers, play a feelings dart gun game, or just start exploring and setting up toys. In my experience, even the most stubborn, determined child gets bored with his own resolve to be sullen after a half hour and starts looking over at what the parents and I are doing. Once he is engaged, I find it is hard for him to leave!

CASE EXAMPLE

Parents Cyndy and Al brought in 6-year-old Mindy who was referred by the parochial school she attended for being unable to sit still or follow directions. At home, she was constantly breaking rules and was overly intrusive with her 2-year-old baby brother Alexander, forcing him to interact with her on her own terms and playing the parent role, taking toys and other objects away from him that he was permitted to have and hitting him when she felt he needed to be "punished." As a result, Alexander was frequently frustrated and crying causing Cyndy to intervene almost constantly. The therapist prepped the parents for the intake in the manner described above and the parents brought in Mindy. When Mindy entered the room, the therapist immediately observed that she "took over" with her energy and natural instinct to pursue whatever interested her rather than the social requirements of the occasion. She flitted from toy to toy, examining it and *quickly discarding it even before there was time for introductions. The therapist observed the parents, Cyndy who was in her early 40's and Al in his early 50's had low energy and their attempts to get Mindy to sit to talk to the therapist from a seated position fell on deaf ears. The therapist saw that more structure was needed and went up to Mindy, going to her level, and asking for eye contact. She told Mindy she had to sit at the table and was given a choice of drawing or playing with Play Doh. Mindy came right over, responding well to strong structuring. At that point, the therapist asked Mindy more about herself and what she liked to do. At one point Mindy got up and started to wander. The therapist asked her what she was doing and she said she needed to find some molds for the dough. She was redirected to sit down while the therapist provided what she asked for. During this exchange, the therapist learned that Mindy liked baking, jumping on the trampo-line, and reading. The therapist asked, "Do you know why your parents brought you here?" Mindy responded in a loud voice, "School." The therapist said, "What about school?" Mindy said, "Sitting." The mother intervened and said that the teachers were concerned that Mindy could not stay in her seat and were disrupt-ing the other children and that she would often not follow directions or rules in school. The therapist asked Mindy, "Does that happen?" Mindy responded, "Yes but only **sometimes.**" The therapist remarked, "I'm glad it's only sometimes and other times you can follow the rules." Mindy added, "But I can't stay in my seat." The therapist then went on to discuss the other issues with the family including Mindy's challenges with her baby brother which she insisted would not be a problem if her baby brother would just listen to her and not bother her. Other background information was obtained until it was clear that Mindy could no longer sit. For the rest of the session the therapist did some family interactive games using the, "I am Proud Ball" to focus attention on personal strengths, counterbalancing the prior focus on problem areas. The therapist also played, "Mother May I," a child's game where one person who plays "mother" stands on one side of the room. The other player lines up on the opposite side of the room. "Mother" tells each player they can take a certain type of step, (e.g., baby step, giant step.) If the player says, "Mother, may I?" they can proceed. If not, they must go back to the beginning. The first player to reach "mother" wins. This was a fun yet very challenging game for Mindy who had to think before she did an action. When the parents played "mother" they were put in a playful structuring role which the therapist thought* *was therapeutic for them. The session ended with the agreement to meet with the parents the following week to finish the assessment and to start some parent training. Mindy was told I would be meeting with her parents next week to figure out a plan to help her in school and how to make things better with her baby brother but that she would come the following week. Mindy asked the therapist if she could play the games again and the therapist agreed.*

The following week the therapist got together with the parents and finished the assessment. She found out that Mindy was adopted at birth and showed signs of high reactivity and impulsivity since she was a baby but little was known or could be obtained about the birth parent. Alexander, somewhat a surprise, was a "last ditch" effort to try to have a biological child, spurred mostly by Mindy's pleas for a sibling. Alexander was such an easy child compared to the very high energy, impulsive, and easily distracted Mindy. Mindy was not aware of her adoptive parentage and the parents were considering when and how to tell her but this was not an issue they wanted to address at present. They also did not want to seek psychiatric services or explore medication for a possible ADHD diagnosis. Along with Mindy's impulsivity came a very high intelligence and despite her distractibility she was doing well in school academically if not behaviorally. They wanted to see if therapy could first address her issues before proceeding to medication.

The following initial goals were set up:

1. *Develop a strong behavior plan in the home to reduce Mindy's tendency to hit, boss and take toys away from her baby brother and teach parents to encourage Mindy to express possible feelings of anger and jealousy toward him verbally so that she would not act out her feelings in an aggressive way.*
2. *Therapist would contact school to see how the school, therapist and parents could work together in achieving school behavioral goals*
3. *Teach coping skills of impulse control through family game play therapy, role plays, and bibliotherapy in the office to be reinforced at home.*

For the remainder of the session the therapist began a parent management training program to teach skills the parents could begin using right away.

Summary

Collaborative treatment planning is an effective way of keeping the child/adolescent and family engaged in treatment and increases the likelihood of successful outcomes. Challenges to creating goals can be met with flexibility and creativity on the part of the therapist. In this initial period, it is important for the clinician to empathize with the caregiver, to educate them about the child's symptoms, to provide choices and options for interventions and to respect the parents' initial decisions about treatment.

CHAPTER 3

Child Disruptive Disorders: Use of Parent Training

• • •

THERAPISTS USING A PAH APPROACH would likely use parent training as a first line intervention for disruptive problems. Parent Training or more specifically Parent Management Training (PMT) has, based on outcome studies, been determined to be an Evidence-Based Intervention (EBI) for children/adolescents with oppositional or conduct disorders. Studies on this approach have been performed for over 20 years with consistently successful results. Michaelson et al. (2013) stated, "PMT is now among the most well established EBI's for child mental health programs with proven benefits in the treatment of child disruptive disorders in a large number of controlled trials." While it is clear that PMT's are evidence-based, studies do not show any measurable differences in effectiveness when compared to each other. Future studies may find different results. (Dretzke et al. 2009).

One well researched program is the Parent Management Training - Oregon Model (PMTO) which uses a social interactional learning model to examine how connections between family members and peers lead to healthy or dysfunctional adjustment (Forgatch & Patterson, 2012). One of the prime focus points of the program is to empower parents to use less coercion in their interactions. Parents are encouraged to focus on strengths, give effective directions, and teach through encouragement. The work is done in either a family format where there is a great deal of flexibility for individualizing the approach or in a group format. All sessions are highly structured and involve role play with the therapist as coach.

Another highly studied approach is the Kazdin Method, or Parent Management Training, PMT, developed at the Yale Parenting Center and Child Conduct Clinic which focuses on training parents to provide positive reinforcement to facilitate change (Kazdin, 2005). The use of prompts, reinforcing through enthusiastic praise, token economy and physical touch are core features of the program. The approach also calls for mild consequence such as time-out or temporary loss of privilege to manage problem behaviors. This method also uses role play extensively and stresses that the therapist herself needs to enthusiastically praise and support the parent for learning new skills. The therapist's use of support, praise, and practice with the parent will reinforce and solidify the parent's ability to change their behavior and implement the skills learned. Today the program combines a problem-solving training module in addition to the parent training to address the needs of the children served at the clinic (Kazdin, 2012).

Other PMT approaches include PCIT, already described in Chapter 1, and *The Incredible Years Training Series* where parents learn through videotapes. In this series, there is a school curriculum and special training is given to teachers (Kazdin, 2005).

There are popular parenting approaches that have good anecdotal evidence among parents, helping professionals, and educators and have been adopted as training guides in facilities for children yet have not had the advantage of being studied in Randomized Controlled Trials (RCT's).[4] One of these is the Nurtured Heart Approach (NHA) originally developed by Howard Glasser almost 20 years ago (Glasser & Easley, 1998; Hektner et. al., 2013). The NHA has been used in Head Start Programs, schools, and foster care agencies among other settings (Ahmann, 2014) and was originally designed for children with disruptive and oppositional disorders. One of the main tenants of the program is to teach parents and teachers to focus their comments, time, attention, and energy, on positive behaviors no matter how small (Ahmann, 2014). The approach was developed based on the observations and experiences Glasser had as a therapist working with families and children with Attention Deficit Hyperactivity

---

4 RCT: A study where people are allocated at random to receive one of several interventions including waitlist or no intervention to compare.

Disorder (ADHD) and Oppositional Defiant Disorder (ODD) and not necessarily on any particular theory or published studies. Despite this, Hektner et. al. (2013) found that most of the elements of the program are strongly aligned with other well researched programs. In addition, there is empirical support for the theoretical underpinnings of the program. A study of 41 NHA Parenting programs where parents completed pre-, post, and follow up surveys showed that parents consistently reported a decrease in yelling, scolding, and responding with positivity. While there were problems in the study design, it did show that the NHA approach was promising as an EBI and should be further studied (Brennan et. al., 2016).

USING A PARENT TRAINING APPROACH: BEGINNINGS

Once a child/adolescent has been identified as having a disruptive disorder, it is important for the therapist to know what the parent has already done to reduce oppositional behavior. There are some interactions parents may identify that have been helpful. For example, a parent might say, "I choose my battles," finding that allowing the child to have a bit more freedom is actually helpful. Looking at what is already working and supporting the parents' efforts are just as important as identifying challenges and less helpful interactions. When parents can enter a training program knowing that the therapist is appreciative of their strengths, they will be more receptive to new information and more confident in their ability to master new skills.

After completing the assessment and identifying some initial goals, it is important for the therapist to do some psychoeducation regarding the efficacy of PMT. Some parents wish the therapist to begin with an approach that has little empirical research data to back it up. For example: Parents Sarah and Mike would like to drop off their 8-year-old son, Avi, who is acting out. They believe that the therapist can get him to "open up" by talking to him individually about why he is so angry. Avi, they believe will then feel better and be more compliant at home. While this may sound logical, research has shown that Avi's symptoms would be more effectively treated by PMT. The therapist can educate the parents regarding the feasibility of trying PMT first, the results of which could initially be seen in a session or two and add additional interventions as needed. It is important here to note that it is likely a disruptive child will still need other types of therapy even when a successful parenting plan is in place and much of the oppositional behavior has been reduced or become manageable. For example, he may struggle with social skills issues, impulsivity, low self-esteem, tendency for negative thinking or difficulty in problem solving. In subsequent chapters, there will be ideas on using PAH approaches to address these difficulties.

Choosing the Method

The therapist, collaborating with the caregiver needs to choose a manualized PMT approach, an adapted approach due to the child's or family's situation or a parent training approach that has the hallmarks of PMT like the NHA but has not been researched in RCT's. An adapted PMT approach may need to be chosen for a variety of reasons. One is that larger families where there are 5 to 10+ sibling or where there are many young children born close together may not be able to implement the components of the manualized program in the manner the approach recommends. For example, a former client of mine, Abby, had 5 children, the oldest and most disruptive was 5-year-old Eli. Abby was able to do much less positive reinforcement and limit setting than typical manualized programs require. Eli's father, who had to work long hours could not be on hand often enough to fill in. The program by necessity, had to be adapted to the needs of the family and what the parents could feasibly accomplish. Another reason for needing to adapt a PMT approach is that a child's co-morbid condition and other family stresses make adherence to the manualized model nearly impossible. For example, Maria and Robert, also parents of 5 children had two with special needs, George age 17 was challenged by high functioning autism and severe mental illness and Cynthia, age 13 was challenged by pervasive developmental disorder, emotion dysregulation disorder, and the family was struggling with her oppositional behavior and wanted to use some parent management strategies. We discovered that behavioral goals, a concept of many PMT's were not useful/realistic for Cynthia because her oppositional behavior was difficult for her to control and quickly led to dysregulation, setting off both her and George. We found it was more useful for the family to determine what they can do to minimize escalation of behavior before Cynthia becomes oppositional. We also discovered that praise, which is also a strong component of PMT's had little effect on shaping Cynthia's behavior. Validation and distraction when possible was more useful to help manage her in a family setting. A third reason for needing to adapt a PMT approach is that the conflicts, trauma and ambivalences within the family are so overwhelming and complex that they may only be able to do a tiny step in the program after weeks of support and encouragement. For example, a parent may be unable to say a kind word to their child or to ever tell them, "No." An example of this instance will be described later in this chapter.

The therapist and caregiver may find that using a parenting method such as NHA that focuses on positive reinforcement for acceptable behaviors and ignoring or providing mild consequence for unacceptable behaviors would be a good alternative. It is possible that a parent had already been through a previous training program such as S.T.E. P., *Systematic Training for Effective Parenting* (Dinkmeyer & McKay, 1983) through their school and would like to continue or had actually been interested in NHA and is excited to learn more about it. Because choice plays a role in determining success in treatment as was discussed in Chapter 1, it is important to consider parent's preferences. Should these methods be chosen, the therapist should keep in mind the importance of practicing new skills in the office with the parent and providing enthusiastic support throughout the process.

The optimal choice when possible is to use a PMT manualized approach. My favorite method is the Kazdin Approach. The case study below will describe how the approach was used to manage ODD as the primary presenting problem and the additional therapies needed for comorbid conditions will be summarized.

CASE EXAMPLE

Matt, a 9-year-old boy who was one of the middle children of 4 siblings had been a difficult child since he was very young. The parents noted something was very different about this child who was easily reactive and unlike the other children as he was unresponsive to the usual discipline and lacked compassion for others, only thinking of his own needs and interests. Most recently he would "blackmail" his family by doing things that would make their life miserable unless he got his way. For example, if he thought one of his siblings touched his Legos in the morning and believed his mother did not provide a severe enough punishment for his unproved allegation he would refuse to get dressed and would procrastinate getting ready for school to the point where the entire family would have to be late for work or school. He knew that his mother would not leave him alone unsupervised so in this way he was aware he had power over the situation and was not concerned how upset and angry other family members were by his behavior. Parents felt consequences for this behavior did not "work" as he either did not care about things that were taken away or he would physically resist doing the consequences he cared about like earlier bedtimes and time-outs. Rewards for good behavior also did not "work" as he was more invested in his idea of personal vengeance and punishing his parents and siblings for not doing his will than getting praise or rewards. In school, he only did well with teachers who were highly structured yet he had frequent episodes where he would be blatantly disrespectful to teachers, and other authority figures and would get detentions or sent to the office for rude comments. He often either did not quite understand what he did wrong in these instances or refused to accept responsibility for any wrongdoing.

Beginning with a PAH approach, the therapist, Jamar, noted to the parents that although their child was highly challenging, there were many strengths in the family including the parents' commitment to helping their child and a willingness to put the time and effort both in the office and at home. The therapist suspected that a strong component of the child's difficulties included ODD yet there seemed to be deficits in social skills and impulse control challenges for which he was currently being medicated.

Jamar observed that the parents were on the right track with trying to implement positive reinforcement and consequence but it was somehow ineffective. He believed that a more systematic, organized approach targeting just a few behaviors and a better incentive plan would have more success and introduced the family to the Kazdin Method (Kazdin, 2005.) The parents agreed to learn more about this approach and apply the principles to the work with their son.[5] While there were many behaviors that needed improving the parents first wanted Matt to improve his morning behavior. Goals and a point system were broken down into the following steps:

1. *Get up without fussing by 8:15 (2 points) or with one reminder (1 point)*
2. *Go to bathroom and brush teeth with no fussing (1 point)*
3. *Get dressed with no fussing or no reminder (1 point)*
4. *Down for breakfast by 8:35 (1 point)*
5. *In car by 8:45 (2 points)*

The parents felt they needed to try something new so they went out of their comfort zone and decided that their child would best be motivated by a monetary reward. Each point would amount to 10 cents which could add up to be spent when he visited his grandparents in 2 weeks.

In the Kazdin method the reward system is simply the "spice" or the extra incentive to help the child become excited about the program. The most important aspect of this method is training the parent to effectively praise the child. The parents were trained to do the following:

1. *Tell Matt exactly what he had done well. For example, "You got up on time, well done!" is preferable to, "Good Boy!" because the former is more specific.*
2. *Remind Matt he is getting a point.*
3. *Use enthusiasm.*

---

5 *For editing purposes, since this case study is a summary of how the Kazdin method was used with this family, some steps were deliberately omitted such as how the family developed the problems and goals for their son. In addition, a few minor adaptations were made from the manualized version of this program to accommodate the clients. For an accurate manualized study of this approach Readers should consult "Parent Management Training" by Alan E. Kazdin.*

4.   *Use physical touch-anything from a pat on the back to a big hug is appropriate for accomplishing the goal.*

The parents were also told that once a pattern is established their son could be rewarded with less frequency until the behavior becomes normalized.

Note: The Kazdin method recommends that the therapist train parents extensively through role play. The method also specifies that parents and children practice goal behaviors in role plays and allow the child to earn points for participating. I find that role playing when practicing any new behavior and skill is invaluable. I have often had the experience where I have been working with a savvy, highly intelligent parent who takes notes and seems completely ready to implement a parenting plan. When I say, "Let's just run through this once for review," doing a simple role play of for example, the "new" way the parent is going to respond to their child challenging a limit, the parent immediately goes right back to their old ineffective way of coping in the role play. My assumption that their interest, enthusiasm, and intelligence would help them make the connection between the theoretical plan and the behavioral implementation is always wrong. How then, can I expect them to try out these new behaviors for the first time when they are in the throes of a stressful situation? Rescue workers, police, soldiers, and fire fighters are given months of role play training in the field so that they are able to react appropriately under stress. When these professionals have done something heroic and are interviewed on television for an act of bravery, they often say, "I remembered my training." As therapists, we should recognize that families are also in need of similar, albeit less intense training, to be able to perform the skill set needed under stress for the behavioral changes they would like to make.

When training the parents, Jamar set up role plays where the parent would have the child practice the goals they just discussed. Initially he played the role of the parent and instructed one of the parents to play the child. The script is as follows:

Therapist *(In the character of the parent): Matt, just for practicing one goal with me, you will get a point. It will just be pretend. Are you ready?*

Parent *(In the character of Matt): OK*
Therapist: *Let's pretend you are going to the bathroom to brush your teeth without fussing but you saw Jimmy (2-year-old brother) was touching your Legos. Do you think you can figure out how to get to the bathroom and still brush your teeth without fussing? Let's try. Here's a box. We'll pretend that's the Legos. And the chair over there is the bathroom.*
Parent: *(Picks up the box) Jimmy is touching my Legos and now he's screaming. (Parent brings the box to the bathroom and then comes out.)*
Therapist: *Matt, you went right in and brushed your teeth without fussing even though you were upset with your brother. You just took the Legos away and told me he was crying. Good Job! (High Five) You get a point!*

Jamar then reviewed the role play and switched roles where he played the child. The parent was encouraged to use the goal sheet and the tips about praise as a guide and Jamar would provide prompts where needed and a great deal of support, praise and encouragement to the parents. The Kazdin method stresses the importance of providing the same praise to parents that they will be using with their own children. This type of praise will encourage them to continue making the behavioral changes needed for the plan to work. *Jamar had the parents come up with other scenarios to help them practice both setting up a role play with their son and praising him when they noticed he accomplished a goal. Jamar continued to play the character of the child throughout the role plays until the parents were more comfortable with the skills.*

Because Jamar suspected that Matt had social skills deficits he recommended that clarity and even bluntness would likely be more effective when introducing this program and the parents agreed. A possible script the family and Jamar drafted was:

"Matt, the family is upset with you for making us late every day for school and work. We want you to be on time and because we know it is so hard for you, we want to reward you. Here's the plan."

The Kazdin Method calls for mild consequence but the family felt that putting in a consequence system was doomed to failure for the reasons mentioned above. They felt that not getting a point was consequence in itself, however they were concerned that their son was so oppositional he would prefer to refuse to participate rather than to earn points for rewards. Jamar and the family decided that if Matt responded in that way, it might be better to have a consequence system as a backup plan because they could then say, "we wanted to reward you for good behavior so you could earn money but OK we will just give you consequences. It's up to you." Having a backup consequence plan was empowering to the parents. Jamar also pointed out that they do not need the child's consent to praise him for good behavior or to "catch" him being good.

In this instance, the child did agree to go with an incentive plan and began to go to school on time more consistently. In a short time, his "refusing to get ready rebellions" were rare and eventually non-existent. In about 3 months the pattern became normalized and the extra rewards were gradually dropped and was sustained by positive verbal reinforcement. Matt's therapy was supplemented by social, problem solving and coping skills training until he achieved greater mastery at home and school.

Some family situations are much more complicated and parents have difficulties with the most rudimentary aspects of behavior management such as saying, "no," or giving any praise for complicated reasons. In these cases, it is better to work more slowly on one incremental change that may possibly take weeks or months to accomplish. The following is a case example of such a difficulty.

Case Example

Marisol, a single parent of daughter, Diana, 10 and son Luis, 5, was struggling with her daughter who suffered from a combination of anxiety and oppositional behavior. The anxiety would manifest itself through excessive worry, episodic school phobia where she refused to go to school, and fussing with homework unless her mother practically gave her all the answers. Her oppositional behavior included refusing to clean up after herself, and going to bed on time which resulted in her over sleeping and being very cranky in the morning. When Diana was refused something she wanted, e.g., a new pack of pencils for school the next day even though the ones she had were working and her mother was extremely tired, she would scream and rave and eventually start throwing objects like pillows at her mother. Her mother would eventually go to the store just to get her to stop and get some peace in the home. Marisol already changed her work hours to go in one half hour later and to leave later so that she can drive Diana late to school as Diana procrastinated and fussed so much. Diana was facing the possibility that she might have to repeat the grade due to so many late arrivals and days missed. Luis felt lonely and left out as so much attention was focused on Diana. At the same time, he appreciated when his mother placated Diana because he just wanted her to stop yelling and carrying on.

Marisol was herself a child of a single parent and described herself as rebellious. Her own mother tended to be critical and highly protective. When at 18, Marisol met a 24-year-old man, Manuel, she became pregnant and against her mother's wishes decided to marry him. Her mother warned her about Manuel whom she felt was "beneath her" and "dangerous" but Marisol finally felt liberated from her mother's criticism and wanted to start her own life. Soon after Diana was born there were signs of trouble, including demeaning remarks about how "fat" she was after giving birth, anger that his supper wasn't ready when she was nursing the baby, and objects flung across the room in anger when he could not find something and assumed she lost it. At first he would apologize but as the years went on, the emotional and physical abuse became worse. The physical abuse escalated to being hit or punched or pushed several times a week in front of pre-school aged, Diana, who would cry and try to protect her mother. The emotional abuse, insults, and name calling became more frequent. When Manuel left after a violent episode she and Diana would cry together, comforting each other.

Marisol was ashamed to tell her mother and blamed her "stubborn pride" for not seeking help sooner. She also did not know where to go or what to do without the financial support of her husband as she could not support herself and her child on her income alone. Finally, the fear of loneliness and being adrift was worse that the fear of the beatings or the effect or her and her daughter. Things came to a head one month after they moved to a new apartment. Hearing an altercation, a neighbor called the police. When the police arrived they saw a 4-year-old child crying on the scene and Child Protective Services was called. Marisol was given a choice: obtain a restraining order and begin to end the cycle of domestic violence or remain in the same situation and the state will seek a foster home placement for Diana. Marisol said that it was only then that she finally realized what she had done to her child and resolved to make it up to her.

It took some weeks to piece together but the therapist realized that the mother was quite incapable of setting reasonable limits due to:

1. *Tremendous guilt over a feeling that it was her fault that Diana suffered so much because her "pride" rendered her unable to get help until she was given an ultimatum.*
2. *A feeling that she needed and should be punished by Diana*
3. *A fear that if she does not give in, Diana will like her father better than her and may eventually want to live with him. (Diana sees her father on alternate weekends when he is available and he tends to spoil her when he sees her.)*
4. *A belief that because Diana was traumatized she should never experience pain or discomfort in any form.*
5. *The fear of how out of out of control Diana would become if she did not have her way.*

In the meantime, Diana often refused to see the therapist. On occasion when the therapist went to the home the child would join for brief periods at the mother's cajoling but then could not be persuaded to come out of her room.

In this instance, the therapist felt that the issue of guilt needed to be addressed in order to move forward. Since Marisol often heard, "It's not your fault, it's the abuser's fault," and found this not to be helpful, the therapist felt that simply acknowledging the mother's painful feelings of guilt was a first step. The therapist asked her if she would like to work on this issue separately in individual work. Marisol was interested but she first wanted to help her daughter. The prospect of her daughter having to repeat a grade was a huge impetus for this mother to acknowledge she needed to change. The therapist pointed out that her guilt may be preventing her from allowing her child to face even the smallest amount of discomfort which is a necessary component to recover from anxiety. Furthermore, in her attempt to create conditions whereby her child could live with little discomfort, she was starting to create another bigger problem. Her child seemed to be learning how to achieve power and control by being abusive. Marisol acknowledged she had already been thinking a great deal about this and how Diana's actions resemble her ex- husband's. The therapist asked Marisol if she would be ready to set a limit with Diana in the spirit of helping Diana challenge her own anxiety. If Diana learned she could "survive" a limit, for example, "No new pencils for tomorrow, we will buy them over the weekend," she will not only learn to stand up to her anxiety, she will learn that she cannot get what she wants by intimidation. Marisol was fearful but said she wanted Diana to complete her own Math homework. She said Diana screams at her to give her the answers but she does not understand how the teachers teach it. Diana changes Marisol's answers anyway so her daughter really does know how to do the assignments. The final plan looked like this:

1. *Marisol would warn Diana in advance that she was not going to help her with Math anymore but if Diana could not do it on her own she would write a note to Diana's teacher so that she would not get in trouble at school. Completing it on her own would earn her points toward a special prize.*
2. *If Diana asked her to do the homework, Marisol would remind her like a broken record that she was not going to do the Math homework with her anymore.*
3. *If Diana started to become agitated, Marisol would change locations, e.g., take Luis outside to play if Diana started becoming agitated and invite her to come. It is likely Diana would not show the same behavior in front of others and may give her time to cool down.*
4. *As a last resort, Marisol would call the Psychiatric Mobile Crisis number especially if Marisol became unusually violent, and would warn Diana of this beforehand.*

The therapist did role plays where she played the parent and Marisol was to play the child responding to the parent's limits about the Math homework. When Marisol played the child, the therapist had the opportunity to see how quickly the child devolved into using guilt, threats, and aggression to manipulate the mother. Then roles were reversed. The role play where the therapist used guilt, threats, and simulated aggression to manipulate the mother, helped Marisol understand what type of stress she would be under if she set a limit. Initially, Marisol was utterly paralyzed in the role play when the therapist said things like, "If you really loved me, you would help me!". Marisol herself needed to become desensitized to her child's manipulation and guilt before she could even successfully complete the role play. On the second try Marisol was much more successful. The role play helped determine what coping skills she would need to draw on when faced with her daughter's stress. Finally, it helped to further refine the strategy the parent would take when finally succeeding in placing a limit on her child.

When the therapist next met with the mother and asked about the plan Marisol said, "It was horrible. We were all crying." Fearing the worst, the therapist asked, "What happened?" Apparently, Diana had a longer than usual homework assignment in Math and demanded that her mother help her, ignoring the previous limit set. Marisol went on to her usual behavior of pleading, screaming, threatening, crying, and eventually throwing sofa pillows and slippers at her mother. Marisol said that she and Luis began crying. She asked Diana, "Why are you doing this to me?" "But," she said, "I stuck to my guns." After about two hours, Diana calmed down and started being nicer and even apologized. In the week following she never asked her mother to help with the Math homework. The therapist felt that a window was finally open toward a path of healing for both the parent and child.

Summary

A PAH approach recognizes that parent training is highly effective in treating disruptive behaviors. It can be used in combination with other treatments for co-morbid conditions or can be adapted for more challenging and complex families. The most important aspect of parent training for the therapist to remember include:

1. Practice the concepts discussed through role play.
2. Provide praise, encouragement and support for any parent's ideas or actions that support effective limit setting and bonding and keep them in the overall plan.
3. Provide creative adaptations where needed while keeping in mind empirical data.
4. Educate and collaborate!

CHAPTER 4

Anxiety

● ● ●

A PAH APPROACH TO A child/adolescent struggling with anxiety would seek to have a strong collaborative relationship with the caregivers both in the office and at home. The advantages to this include:

1. The therapist can design opportunities for the child to be better understood by the parent.
2. Both parent and child can learn about the nature of the child's anxiety and how it affects his functioning together.
3. The parent can help the child practice skills learned in the office at home.
4. The parent(s) can design a support plan to help the child reinforce new behaviors, e.g., going to school consistently, reduced checking behavior, using positive self-talk, etc.
5. The parent is frequently a "first responder" as the child frequently does not get triggered during his weekly therapy appointment but just before school, at bedtime, during homework or at midnight during a nightmare. Working collaboratively will help the caregiver(s) develop the skills and competence they need to manage their child's anxiety. It also allows the therapist the opportunity to provide support to enable the parents to cope with the stress of their anxious child and to make the changes needed in order for him to thrive.

Combining a collaborative approach with the caregiver with the principles of cognitive behavioral therapy (CBT) and exposure response prevention

(ERP) can be a highly effective way to treat anxiety. Research shows that CBT and ERP significantly improves anxiety in children and adolescents (Read et al, 2013; Davis & Whiting, 2011, Kendall et all, 2012). Further studies indicate that working with the family using these modalities have some advantages over individual approaches. For example, in a meta-analysis, Carr (2014) found that family work is more effective than individual therapy for school refusal for school phobia and that CBT treatments for anxiety are at least as effective as individual treatments when done in a family setting, more effective if one of the parents suffers from anxiety and are overall more effective in improving family functioning. Another interesting research study by Smith et al. (2014) points to the importance of the caregiver. In this program the caregiver only was given treatment to help their child with an anxiety disorder diagnosis. Parents were engaged as collaborators in a ten-week program and provided with psychoeducation and CBT based treatments as well as parent/child tasks to complete between sessions. Researchers found that after completing a 10-week program, there were decreases in the number of anxiety disorder diagnoses, parent's rating of their child's anxiety impairment, and the clinician's rating of the severity of the child's anxiety compared to waiting list clients. This study, while not conclusive does indicate the importance and significance of parent-child home-based treatments.

For those readers unfamiliar with the concepts of CBT or ERP or as it is sometimes called, exposure therapy, I would recommend reading, "Cognitive Behavioral Play Therapy for Children with Anxiety and Phobias," by Knell & Dasari in *Short Term Play Therapy for Children with Anxiety and Phobias*, edited by Kaduson and Schaefer (2006). Here, I will summarize the concepts of CBT and exposure therapy below as well as other therapies used to treat anxiety such as psychoeducation, relaxation training, mindfulness, and Dialectical Behavior Therapy (DBT). Through the case study I will demonstrate how therapists can provide a variety of play based treatments where parents are a dynamic part of the approach.

The theory behind CBT is that a stimuli or event triggers thoughts and those thoughts trigger feelings which lead to reactions (Bourne, 2005).

For example, a child who raised their hand in class three times was not picked on by her teacher (**stimuli**). She **thought,** "My teacher hates me." She left class **feeling** upset and sad and then made fun of a shy unpopular child to elevate herself (**reaction.**) This **reaction** resulted in another peer telling her to stop which made her feel worse about herself and even more angry. Another child could have experienced the same event or stimuli. She **thought,**" I guess the teacher wanted other kids who don't usually talk to answer." She left class **feeling** calm and actually forgot about the event, enjoying the rest of her day. CBT attempts to help clients change irrational thoughts about events or stimuli that lead to excessive fears, anger, or depression. In the first example, we are assuming the child did not have enough evidence from the event or prior to the event to assume that the teacher "hated" her and the therapy would work on challenging those assumptions in a variety of ways. Use of logic, checking whether in fact the assumptions are valid and challenging faulty beliefs are some ways of challenging cognitions. With children, this is done in a play-based way and is called Cognitive Behavioral Play Therapy, CBPT.

The clinician should be careful not to confuse a cognitive distortion with adaptive anxiety. For example, clinicians new to CBT or trauma work have asked questions similar to the following: "The Smith Family, especially Mrs. Smith, is afraid every time they walk out of the door of their home. This has occurred since Mr. Smith, who was abusive, was released from jail. How can I apply CBT so that they won't be so scared?" In this case, their anxiety and fear may be an adaptive response and may be an indicator that the family needs more information about Mr. Smith's whereabouts and a good safety plan. Mrs. Smith may need to consult with her local police on how to stay safe. Distinguishing between adaptive anxiety and cognitive distortions due to an anxiety disorder is important and helps determine the most effective interventions.

Another aspect of managing anxiety is ERP. In this therapy, the client is gradually exposed to the stimuli they are avoiding with supports and prevented from responding in their usual maladaptive ways by, for example avoiding or running from the stimuli or using any number of compulsive behaviors like checking, washing, or performing rituals. A parent telling his school phobic child that he can no longer stay home from school but has to at least stay for morning classes is a type of ERP. A support plan to ease the child into the classroom with built in rewards for bravery developed by the guidance counselor will help the plan be successful and help prevent the child from lapsing into his old ways of coping by, for example, demanding to be allowed to go home. Exposure treatments are often included in CBPT or other CBT based treatment plans especially when avoidance is used as a primary coping mechanism.

Psychoeducation is a cornerstone of many successful CBT based programs to treat anxiety and is likely the first step a child may encounter (Read et al. 2013). Psychoeducation helps a child understand the nature of his diagnosis, how anxiety is influencing his cognitions and how CBT, ERP and other coping skills such as relaxation training and mindfulness can work to help him return to normal functioning. If medication has been prescribed or is being considered, the therapist can collaborate with the parent on how best to present the information to the child.

A frequent component of treatment programs to reduce anxiety includes relaxation training. For example, the highly studied and efficacious "Coping Cat" program for anxious children includes a section on relaxation in addition to CBT, problem solving and additional coping skills training. (Albano & Kendall, 2002; Kendall et al, 2012). There appears to be few published RCT studies regarding the effect of relaxation training on anxiety compared to the myriad of studies on CBT however, Tercelan et al. (2015) found that teaching relaxation techniques to people with anxiety disorders enhances psychological and pharmacological treatments. Some examples of simple exercises that work with children and adolescents include belly breathing, tensing and relaxing muscles, or visualizing relaxing or anxiety free scenes like vacations.

Dialectical and Behavior Therapy originally created by Dr. Marsha Linehan for Borderline adults, (Linehan, 1993) is being adapted for children with some success (Perepletchikova et al., 2011). DBT is an intervention that teaches a series of coping skills in a supportive environment. Children with anxiety can especially benefit from the Distress Tolerance module where a child learns to tolerate severe stress through distraction or self-soothing using their senses. Other modules include Mindfulness, Emotion Regulation, and Interpersonal Effectiveness.

Mindfulness, outside of the DBT module is considered an intervention on its own and is quite well known in popular culture. I recently took a survey of Apps available for purchase on my phone with the word, "Mindfulness" in it and I came up with 22 in one minute! Because using mindfulness with the clinical population, especially children and adolescents, is relatively newer than CBT there are fewer published studies. Several that have been done show that it is a promising intervention (Semple et al. 2009; Semple et al, 2005.) In a review of 9 studies comparing mindfulness and acceptance-based treatments (MABT) with CBT for social anxiety disorder (SAD), authors, Norton et al. (2015) concluded that while CBT continues to be a first line treatment for SAD, MABT shows promise in the treatment of other anxiety disorders. They also commented that it may be an effective alternative for those who are not responsive to CBT.

The following case study will demonstrate an integrated and collaborative intervention using a PAH approach for a highly anxious school phobic child. Interventions will include psychoeducation, CBT, ERP, Distress Tolerance, adapted from the DBT module, relaxation training and mindfulness using play-based approaches. In office parent roles include participant in CBPT and activities to teach coping skills, provider of bibliotherapy and supportive listener for psychoeducation. Home-based roles include implementer of ERP plan, coping skills coach, and provider of positive reinforcement for coping behaviors.

CASE STUDY

Mandy was a 9-year-old intelligent child who was the second oldest of 4 siblings, the youngest being one-year-old. She came from an in-tact family and did not experience any prior traumas or major losses. Neither of the parents, Jim and Martha, experienced anxiety yet the paternal grandmother was reported to be highly anxious throughout her life and was presently taking medication for anxiety prescribed by her M.D. Mandy was always more anxious than her siblings.

She had difficulty especially adjusting to school and many new experiences. For example, she would cling to her mother, refusing to go to kindergarten until the teacher intervened and led her away. She would cry and get very scared if, for example, the firemen came to school to teach about fire safety. Teachers learned to carefully prepare and prep Mandy for new experiences and give her a choice about whether to attend. Mandy also seemed to worry about things her other siblings never thought of, e.g., whether her parents would die, if her bike would get stolen or if someone would steal her. Her parents handled her fears by reassuring her and providing distraction which seemed to help.

At the time of therapy Mandy became school phobic after an extended school vacation. The parents would send her to school but she was so upset they would drop her off in the guidance office. If the guidance counselor managed to get her to class she would shortly start crying. Crying in the presence of classmates made her embarrassed and she would go to the nurse where she would call her mother and tearfully ask to be picked up. The private school Mandy attended said they could not handle a school related anxiety of this magnitude and told the parents she would need to have counseling and the school staff would need to consult with the child's counselor to develop a school plan if she were to remain in school.

When Mandy came to therapy she had not been to school for three days. Upon further exploration there was no particular incident Mandy or the parents could identify that triggered this bout of school phobia other than the extended vacation and that Mandy usually finds going to school difficult. Mandy explained that she gets nervous and sad in school because, "I miss my Mommy," and "I feel homesick."

In this case, the therapist shortened the intake and goal setting process so that some basic psychoeducation and early planning could begin at the first session. In a psychoeducation session, the goal is to be informative yet positive and with children, making it participatory and fun is key. In Mandy's case, the therapist's, Mrs. L's script is as follows:

Mrs L: *I'd like to pause a minute and tell Mandy about what I think she is experiencing because I think she will understand it better. Is that OK with you? (to parent, Martha)*

Mandy, you have something called "anxiety." That is good news and bad news. The bad news is that it is very painful. The good news is that it is something very treatable which means we can do things to make it go away. One of those things is to teach you everything I know about anxiety and all the ways people get helped by it and you will find out which ways help you the best. Mandy, If you were a soldier in combat and were afraid of being killed, does that make sense?

Mandy: *(looking at mother) Yes?*

Mrs. L: *Great answer! Does it make sense that you would be nervous that you would fail a really hard test your forgot to study for?*

Mandy: *Yes*

Mrs. L: *Does it make sense that if you were going to the grocery store with your mother that you would be nervous that a gigantic earthquake would swallow you up in the parking lot?*

Mandy: *(Giggling) No.*

Mrs. L: *No it doesn't make sense but that's what anxiety tends to do. It tricks us into thinking there's danger or gloominess or hardship where it is not very likely to happen.*

Do you have an alarm clock?

Mandy: *No*

Mrs. L: *How do you get up for school?*

Mandy: *My Mom wakes me.*

Mrs. L: *So, your Mom is your alarm clock. What time does she get you up?*

Mandy: *7:30*

Mrs. L.: *What if your Mom's timing became off and she began waking you up at 4:00 and then at 6:00. Would that be good?*

Mandy *(looking at mother and giggling) Terrible!*

Mrs. L.: *That's also how anxiety is. Like an alarm going off at the wrong time giving you feelings that don't go with the situation so when you feel nervous and homesick at school—that's anxiety knocking on your brain at the wrong time. Do you remember when you weren't so nervous?*

Mandy: *I guess…*

Parent: *Do you remember a few months ago when you were telling me to hurry so you wouldn't be late for school?*

Mandy: *That was because there was a spelling bee which was FUN.*

Mrs. L.: *If there was a spelling bee now would your anxiety go away just like that and you could go to school?*

Mandy: NO!

Mrs. L.: *So the anxiety has gotten too strong in your brain. We are going to learn ways you can make the anxiety weaker so you can be more in control how does that sound?*

Mandy: Good.

Mrs. L. *The very first tool I am going to teach both of you is exposure. Has anyone ever heard the saying, "If you fall off a bicycle, get right back on?"*

Parent: *Yes.*

Mrs. L.: *What does it mean?*

Mandy: *Get on it right away because if you wait you will be too scared 'cause you will be afraid you'll fall.*

Mrs. L.: *Exactly. Anxiety gets stronger when someone waits to face what they are afraid of or avoids facing what they are afraid of. The more they avoid, the "scarder" they become, so the longer you don't attend school, Mandy, the harder it will be to go back. But you HAVE to go back to school.*

Parent: *That's right*

Mandy: *(Getting teary)*

Mrs. L.: *But exposure doesn't mean all at once, because all at once doesn't work for anxiety. So, I don't mean go back to school all day with no plan. I know this is scary but we need to come up with a plan, even if it is just to go to the school to collect your assignments and talk to the guidance counselor at first. That will help you little by little get exposed to the school. We will also work on skills here too to help you feel less anxious.*

Parent: *Can you call the school?*

Mrs. L: *I can call them with our idea for our beginning plan. How are you doing Mandy?*

Mandy: *I Don't want to go back to school!*

Mrs. L: *I know this is very, very scary and your will miss your Mommy and the anxiety is very strong right now.*

Parent: *Mandy, you can't miss too many more days of school or you will have to repeat the grade. Mrs. L is trying to help. Like she said we will figure out a plan little by little where I will come with you so you are not so scared at first.*

Mandy: *You'll come with me?*

Parent: *Yes at first. Is that OK? (to Mrs. L.)*

Mrs. L.: *Of course. We'll start by giving Mandy the support she needs to make the steps she had to take. Let's play a little game. Mandy, imagine you are walking up to the school door. What kinds of nervous or sad thoughts are in your mind? I am going to use them for my anxiety puppet character.*

Mandy: *I don't want to go to school. I miss my Mommy. I want to go home. I'm afraid I'll cry. I'll be embarrassed.*

Mrs. L.: *Great. (Mrs. L writes down Mandy's words in order and 5 separate responses. She gives the responses to Mandy.)*

Now we are going to play a game. I am going to play the part of Anxiety with this Puppet (which is a flamboyant dinosaur). For every sentence I say, I want you to say the following response in a voice louder than mine: [6]

Mrs. L: *(As Anxiety Dinosaur) YOU DON'T WANT TO GO TO SCHOOL!*

Mandy: *I don't have to listen to you. (reading off paper)*

Mrs. L.: *(coaching) You have to say the sentence louder than my voice was.*

Mandy: *I DON'T HAVE TO LISTEN TO YOU!*

Mrs. L: *Good. (As Anxiety Dinosaur) YOU WILL MISS YOUR MOMMY!!*

Mandy: *SO WHAT!*

Mrs. L: *YOU WANT TO GO HOME!*

Mandy: *EVERYONE DOES!*

Mrs. L.: *YOU ARE AFRAID YOU WILL CRY!*

Mandy: *I'LL GO TO THE NURSE!*

Mrs. L.: *YOU'LL BE EMBARASSED!!!*

Mandy: *GET A LIFE!!! (Giggles)*

The game was then repeated with Mindy practicing walking up to the pretend door of the school with her mother by her side.

After this game Mandy felt more relaxed and empowered knowing that her mother would be with her and that she could "talk back" to anxiety. She felt that she could go to one class if her mother could walk her in and sit in the guidance office. After going to class, she would come back and check with her mother who would either leave for work and return to pick her up at lunchtime and take her

---

6 This game can also be played where the child makes up his/her own comebacks to their own fear thoughts

home or leave and take her home after her first class. For every hour of school Mandy would make it through, she would receive a monetary reward toward something she really wanted. The therapist wrote a note for the school the next day.

The report from the mother by phone the next day was that Mandy was extremely scared and almost did not get out of the car to walk up to school. When she did, she refused to enter the classroom so the mother sought out the guidance counselor with Mandy and my note in hand to discuss the situation yet the guidance counselor was not in. Fortunately, the nurse was in and she convinced Mandy to attend one class. Mandy, however, did not last until the afternoon but her mother thought that it was possibly partly due to a history test being scheduled the next period. Martha confided to Mrs. L. that she did not have too many days when she could attend work late. Mrs. L. said that Mandy would need to know her limitations and that another plan would have to be made if she could not stay at least until lunchtime soon. Mrs. L reminded the mother to be very positive about Mandy's achievements and let her know that she would learn more skills next time so that going to school would be less painful. There was also an option to explore the benefits of medication through having the daughter obtain a psychiatric evaluation. The parents decided to wait at this juncture and focus on skills.

By the next session the therapist had been able to speak with school staff and found they were very cooperative and willing to do anything to help Mandy whom they saw as a well behaved intelligent and sensitive child. They were willing to go along with the gradual exposure plan and the guidance counselor was willing to put in a school incentive plan for every hour of class attended. Mandy was "making it' through to 12:15 and bringing home work for the afternoon classes yet was frequently visiting the guidance counselor who was allowing her to come if she felt nervous or like she would cry. Mandy could spend 3 visits per morning in the guidance office for up to 15 minutes at a time yet was not crying or running to the nurse.

Mrs. L. felt that skills focusing on relaxation training, mindfulness and CBT could be key in helping Mandy reduce her anxiety which would hopefully lengthen her school day and reduce her visits to the guidance office. One of the activities was to have the parent or child read the first chapter in What to do When You Worry Too Much *by Dawn Huebner, PhD., and do the workbook activities together. The first chapter playfully describes how the more one thinks anxious thoughts, the greater they become, using a creative and funny metaphor. It is an easy way to put the parent in a healing role and to introduce a child friendly curriculum for anxiety based on CBT skills. The first chapter teaches children the concept of how excessive rumination can make anxiety worse. Mrs. L. took concepts in the workbook and expanded on them after they were introduced. One activity was that Mrs. L. had Mandy write down a few anxious thoughts on separate pieces of paper. For example, Mandy wrote, "What if my mother forgets to pick me up?" Mrs. L then had Mandy scrunch the thought up into a paper ball. She then threw it to Mandy so she could "catch" the anxious thought. Mandy then announced a distracting thought or activity which had been previously discussed and got to make a "basket" into the garbage bin.*

Using Distress Tolerance, Relaxation, and Mindfulness

*Mrs. L. taught Mandy and parent how the brain works. She asked Mandy to point to her forehead and explained that the front part of her brain is called the frontal lobe. The frontal lobe, she explained is the part of the brain that tells us how to solve problems, enables us to learn at school and helps us to figure out what to do when we are stressed out. She then asked Mandy to point to the back of her upper neck. She explained that this is the brain stem and when people become stressed, anxious, or angry, special chemicals from this area start forming and flooding the whole brain. These chemicals are called dopamine and norepinephrine and when their levels become too high, the frontal lobe, the part of our brain that helps us figure out how to reason things out actually turns OFF! The back of our brain which is filled with panic and fear takes over! But enzymes "eat up" the excess chemicals so that our frontal lobe which helps us solve problems can turn on again.[7] * (It can be fun to do a demonstration or a multisensory enactment of how the brain shuts down and turns on again. I like to make the enzymes look like "PAC MEN" who ferociously gobble up the excess chemicals.)*

This is why, Mrs. L. went on to explain, that you freeze up when you are about to enter the school and have difficulty staying in class even for the morning.

---

7 A great explanation of this phenomenon is in an article in Scientific American entitled, "This is Your Brain in Meltdown," April 2012.

Despite all the skills you have learned, like logic, talking back to the anxiety, using distraction, you cannot use them because your frontal lobe is turned OFF and you need to wait for the enzymes to work to turn it on again. But, she added, there are things people can do to help their frontal lobes turn on a bit faster:

Mrs. L taught the following skills over the weeks of therapy that Mandy and her mother learned together.

1. *Change the body temperature, a DBT skill. Mrs. L. recommended that Mandy bring a little wet towel with an ice cube in a container to school so that she can put it on her face to help cool down her overall body temperature or to simply ask to get a drink of water.*

2. *Mrs. L and family had a discussion about a possible scent which would be soothing to Mandy. For example, bringing a sprig of eucalyptus she could crush in her hand and smell might help calm her down until she could think straight. (DBT Distress tolerance skill.)*

3. *Since touch can be soothing as well, Mrs. L. brought out a variety of objects for Mandy to touch including Play Doh and squishy balls, smooth beach stones, and a bean bag. Mandy chose her favorite "touch" and Mrs. L asked mother if Mandy could take it home as a soothing transitional object.*

4. *Belly breathing- Breathe 5 counts in and 8 counts out. Mandy and parent had fun practicing this. Mrs. L. introduced the concept of belly breathing by initially having the pair slouch in their chair with their hands crossed over their stomach to feel the belly rise and fall. When they slowly sat up they should feel the same sensation.*

5. *Mrs. L taught some of the basics of mindfulness through meditation. To introduce the concepts, she distributed Play Doh to both Mandy's parent and Mandy. She instructed them to get comfortable. In a soft and soothing voice, she directed them to take deep breaths while focusing their attention on the feel and texture of the Play Doh. If other thoughts wandered in she instructed them to observe the thoughts and allow them to pass though their minds, focusing again on the feeling, texture, smell, shape, etc. of the Play Doh. This activity was ended after 2 or 3 minutes. Mandy enjoyed this activity very much and her mother also found*

it relaxing. Martha thought it would help calm Mandy down at night. Mrs. L. directed them to several Apps they could obtain on Martha's phone which had 5 minute meditations that parent and child could listen to together and practice.

By the end of 10 weeks, Mandy was attending class regularly yet her trips to the guidance office continued to be excessive. A structured plan suggested by Mrs. L. in conjunction with the school to limit the time and frequency of the trips worked well. The final plan was that Mandy would be given 3 passes per day to see the guidance counselor for no more than 10 minutes at a time. If she did not need all 3 passes she could collect what she did not use. Once she collected 12, the guidance counselor would take her out for lunch. Mandy found she was stronger than she realized and collected her 12 passes in less than 2 weeks.

Within 5 months' time Mandy was able to bring her anxiety down to a manageable level as she continued to practice and develop skills to cope with her anxiety. Her mother became adept in understanding how best to be helpful to her daughter.

SUMMARY

It is hoped that the reader is beginning to get a sense of how to structure techniques such as psychoeducation, relaxation training, distress tolerance, mindfulness, bibliotherapy, and CBT so that the parent is frequently in a supportive, interactive or playful role with the child. The work that is done in the office is often a "springboard" for the work the caregiver(s) and child can continue in the home. While the case example described a PAH intervention with a child, it has been my experience that anxious adolescents appreciate learning about their anxiety and developing skills in a parent/child setting and even enjoy some of the playful ways of learning skills. With teens, there is usually some time that needs to be devoted to interpersonal issues that have evolved between parent and child and adding a parent training component to increase positivity helps to ease friction. A beneficial "side effect" of this work is increased bonding between parent and child and an increased feeling of competency in the parent.

CHAPTER 5

Trauma

● ● ●

"IT TAKES A VILLAGE TO raise a child," is an old adage yet it describes the thinking behind working with children/adolescents with a PAH approach. A PAH clinician seeks to involve the caregiver, family and community where relevant and possible in the intervention plan. The inspiration for this comes in great measure from the findings of Dr. Bruce Perry, developer of the *Neurosequential Model of Therapeutics* who has researched child trauma since the 1990's. Perry's research indicates that the brain develops from the bottom, where the brainstem occurs, to the top at the cortex. The lowest region of the brain, developed in infancy and early childhood regulates body temperature and heart rate (Sori & Schnur, 2014). Moving up to the mid brain or the diencephalon is the area that manages sleep and arousal. The limbic is the next layer which handles the ability to regulate emotions and develop attachment and at the top is the cortex which houses executive function like verbal ability and problem solving. Perry's research found that the higher regions of the brain depend on effective input from the lower regions in order to develop successfully. When impairment in the lower region is caused by trauma or severe neglect, it can adversely affect the upper regions (Perry 2009). Areas such as speech, language, communication, and attachment can be affected. Perry's *Neurosequential Model of Therapeutics* seeks to map out the deficits in the brain affected by the trauma so that more comprehensive services can be provided by schools, caregivers, and community centers. A PAH clinician recognizes the complexity of deficits that may already have occurred and would seek to network with the community and caregiver to address these issues.

Perry found that severely traumatized children have impairments in the ability to regulate emotions which is an impairment in the lower brain and, until they can go on to other tasks requiring higher brain functions such as communication, processing, etc., it is important to help them learn to regulate themselves. His research consistently shows that patterned repetitive sensory activities help the brain to self-regulate (Perry,2008). These may include drumming, music, movement, yoga, or a parent's rhythmic rocking of a child. Here a PAH approach would place a high priority in coaching a parent to soothe or deescalate a triggered child.

Perry also discovered that human interconnectedness is a powerful force in a child's ability to heal from trauma. He states (2006), "Ultimately what determines how children survive trauma physically, emotionally, or psychologically is whether people around them-- particularly the adults they should be able to trust and rely upon—stand by them with love, support, and encouragement" (p.5). Because attachment is such a strong predictor of healing, the PAH therapist attempts to strengthen the parent/child bond throughout the therapeutic process.

Other researchers such as Van der Kolk also point to the importance of attachment and bonding in mitigating the devastating impact a trauma could have on a child. Van der Kolk (2005) states that traumatized children have difficulty with emotion regulation. Without secure attachment from their caregiver they will be excessively anxious, angry and have a chronic yearning to be cared for.

Goldfinch (2009) notes that traumatized children who have difficulty regulating emotion may become triggered quickly. This triggering may be confusing for the adults like teachers and parents who care for them as even positive events like birthday parties may trigger a negative reaction. A PAH therapist recognizes that much of the "therapy" may not occur in the office when the child is likely regulated but instead may occur at home, in school or in the community when the child is triggered. The PAH clinician recognizes that much of the work may be to help the child be understood by his support system in the home and community and to give them the tools they need to help the child navigate their world. For example, a component of the therapy may be to teach the caregiver to provide patterned repetitive activities like rocking or singing to calm their child or to listen to the angry raving of their adolescent rather than cutting them off into sullen silence.

Another aspect of the work is encouraging where possible family processing of the traumatic event or series of events, Processing, which is recalling events and tolerating negative emotions in a supportive setting, is a strong component of trauma focused cognitive behavioral therapy (TFCBT). This approach has been recognized as an effective therapy according to numerous studies (Prather & Golden, 2009). In a PAH approach, there is a recognition that frequently all family members have been affected in some way by the traumatic event or series of events and starting a family processing can be a dynamic beginning to treatment. In addition, a family or caregiver/child processing can help facilitate understanding and thus increase the ability of the caregiver to be responsive to the child. As mentioned above, caregiver's attunement and responsiveness is considered essential in the child's ability to heal from trauma. If the clinician observes that the parent has difficulty in the session responding in an empathic way to the child, he has the ability to address it by: 1) providing extra support to the parent for her own needs 2) offer parent guidance, or 3) recommend specific parent/child attachment therapy such as *Theraplay®*.

Frequently there are traumatic events that leave families without basic needs such as food, clothing, shelter, or safety. It is essential that the family is aware that those needs are being addressed before other issues can be on the table. At times those concerns wax and wane as for example, a housing issue that was thought to be stable suddenly becomes unsafe. With those families, strong case management services may be even more important than therapy services until basic needs are met. Below are case examples, one of which needed extensive case management in addition to therapy services and others describe whole family processing of traumatic events.

CASE EXAMPLE- FAMILY PROCESSING OF DEATH BY HOMICIDE
Suzanne, a family therapist worked with a mother, Pearl, and her three teen-aged daughters, Natalee, Shamika, and Renay after Pearl's husband and father

to the three girls was killed in an armed robbery at a convenience store. Initially Suzanne did a processing with a feelings thermometer. She made columns and at the top labeled them with specific emotions including happy, sad, angry, scared, embarrassed, guilty, hopeful, confused, and other. She instructed each member to fill in how much of each feeling they were experiencing regarding the murder of their loved one. If they were experiencing strong feelings of one particular emotion they would fill it close to the top and if they felt it only a little they would fill it closer to the bottom. Feelings that did not apply would be skipped. She then asked if anyone would be willing to share their feelings thermometers with the others and if they did, she would ask questions like, "I see you filled "angry" all the way to the top. What makes you the angriest about this?" After the family processing, Suzanne realized that while there was a great deal of grief, there was also tremendous rage, and a sense of helplessness in the rage. For the next session, Suzanne brought out a big piece of mural paper. In the middle, she wrote the words, "IT SUCKS!" which was a popular expression for teens at the time meaning anything from, "It's not fair," to "It's horrible." She invited the teens and their mother to either write words, draw pictures or symbols or paste images from magazines on the mural to express their feelings. The teens enjoyed the activity and through using the were able to express their anger in a visual creative form. Natalee wrote a letter to the killer on the mural describing her feelings of anger and grief while her older sister Renay drew a symbol of a heart being torn apart. Others wrote or cut out words or phrases like, "sadness," "I miss you," "HOPE" or expressions of outrage like, "Stay in jail FOREVER!" When the activity was completed Suzanne felt a lessening of tension in the room and the family reported to her that the intervention was helpful. Suzanne was aware there was a great deal more to process but that a milestone was reached in the healing.

Case Example of Multiple Trauma[8]

Ana had come from her country of origin in Central America to escape from gang violence after a gun was put to her head in an attempt to extort money from

---

8 Ana agreed to share her story provided identifying information was changed to protect confidentiality.

her. Ana knew that, although she was not killed this time, she was marked by the gang and she and her children would no longer be safe. She felt her only choice to escape being killed was to leave to America where her husband had immigrated years before. She left on foot with her 9-year-old son, Jose, leaving her 3-year-old daughter, Marisol hidden with relatives well within the interior and hopefully out of reach of the gangs until she could send for her. After harrowing experiences crossing several central American countries she was dropped off at the US Border by a guide and left there alone with her son in the wilderness where they were pursued by wolves for hours until the Border Patrol picked them up and jailed them for a month. Their deportation was postponed because her husband and brother were here and posted bail for her and her son and she was granted a hearing, hoping for asylum. When she reunited with her husband she had been hopeful of a new life yet quickly learned that he was physically abusive yet felt powerless to do anything but to take it. It was during an extremely violent episode where she almost lost her life that neighbors called the police and Ana was taken to a domestic violence shelter and Child Protective Services became involved.

It was at this time that Jose revealed he had been sexually molested by his father on several occasions.

When Jose came to see Maria, a therapist who worked in an agency that was able to provide both case management and therapy services, he was having daily nightmares and was wetting his bed. He did not want to see his father and could not sleep at night. Ana was having panic attacks, anxiety, depression and had no hope.

Maria had the first session with Ana alone where she processed her sadness about the abuse as she loved her husband and had hoped things would work out between them. Ana mostly cried during the initial session and frequently in subsequent sessions. In the next session, Maria met with Ana and Jose, telling Jose she had been speaking with her mother about what happened but would like to hear about it in his works. Jose readily opened up and this is when the entire story described above yet in much greater detail was told. Martha felt that their trauma was such that it needed to be processed multiple times to more fully process the feelings connected to the various aspects of the traumas experienced. She used games like, "Exploring My World," (Childswork/Childsplay), "Thoughts and Feelings Cards," (Bright Spot Publishers) and feelings thermometers, described above to stimulate expression of feelings and further processing. As she did these family games more of the feelings of fear and rage as well as hope and determination were expressed.

At one point, Jose said he was having nightmares about his father touching him in his private parts. Maria discovered that Jose continued to experience this as highly traumatic and stressful and possibly accounted in part for the bedwetting. In addition to helping Jose further process his rage which was his predominant feeling over the incidents, Maria thought she could help Jose have some control over the nightmares. She brought in an adult coloring book and mother, Martha, and Jose colored a picture. Jose found it very relaxing and Maria gave her the coloring book and instructed her to color one page before bed. Jose did so and due to a more relaxed state of mind upon sleeping, the nightmares and bed wetting stopped.

Maria's work was supplemented by an entire team of services which provided case management for legal advocacy to obtain a permanent restraining order and residency status, housing, adequate food, after school activities, employment assistance, etc. Maria also provided some individual sessions to Ana to process her grief and despair and to help connect her to her natural strength which was her determination to change her circumstances. Child guidance to help Ana feel more competent when Jose was triggered especially by reminders of his father further empowered Ana as a parent. An intern who was able to work on Sundays made home visits to the homeless shelter where Ana and Jose resided to show them how to use the buses, take them to a nearby park and spend some time with them to reduce their general sense of loneliness and isolation.

After almost a year of therapy and case management both Ana and Jose had greatly improved and their outlook on life was hopeful. Ana was no longer feeling depressed and anxious but was more positive. She obtained her residency after a long legal struggle and was learning to speak English. She also obtained housing and employment and will be able to legally bring her daughter over to be with her in the future. Jose was no longer feeling anxious and had processed much of his anger. He was obtaining excellent grades at school with aspirations to become a lawyer to help women in his mother's position so, he said, "They do not have to cry so much."

TRAUMA FAMILY PROCESSING THROUGH THE CREATIVE ARTS

The creative arts provide a means of expression that cannot be easily accessed in words.

Rubin (2006) states, "A massive shock to the system.... elicits powerful feelings for which words are inadequate, yet image, sound, movement, and story can offer a welcome release. The arts help both to *express* and to *contain* otherwise overwhelming emotions" (p. 10). Although there have been limitations in the research on using the creative arts to heal trauma due to the flawed designs in the studies thus far, (Van Westrhenen, N. & Fritz, F. 2014), the use of the arts enables therapists to more effectively engage children in affect expression, emotion regulation, and mastery. (Crenshaw, 2006).

CASE EXAMPLE: FAMILY PROCESSING USING ART

Johnny, an art therapist was working with a family with 3 young children. He noticed that the two oldest, ages, 4 and 6, would set the dolls up in a bed and stab them with the Play Doh knife and then stab Johnny, himself. He realized they were doing a reenactment of the trauma they experienced when their father came in through a window in a drunken rage and started stabbing their mother while they were in bed with her.

Johnny sensed the children needed a way to externalize the situation to more easily process their feelings about the incident. He had everyone participate in the drawing in a picture of a monster. The children quickly identified that the "monster" would be their father. The "monster" was then hung up on the wall and the children were instructed to say anything they wanted to it. The children said things like, "Why did you do that to us?" "Why did you hurt Mommy?" "I hate you!" "I hope you stay in jail forever!"

When they were finished, Johnny took a fat black marker and showed the children how to draw lines over the "monster" to signify the lines of the jail cell where the father was currently incarcerated. After the activity, the relief, Johnny said, in the air was palpable and he felt one milestone had been crossed in the family's road to healing.

Summary

Because the research regarding the importance of caregiver attunement and stability in mitigating the effects of trauma on the child the PAH therapist would make every effort to treat the family as a whole to encourage stability in the caregiver/child relationship. This is done in several ways including:

1. Assess the degree to which attachment may be affected and provide services and support to restore the parent's ability to effectively care for the child.
2. Process traumatic events where possible as a family to begin to facilitate a greater degree of understanding and empathy.
3. Understand that much of the "therapy" may take place outside the office when the child is dysregulated. Coach the parent with the skills they need to cope with their child's triggers and provide ancillary support such as individual therapy to help them with their own stress as they navigate this process.
4. Make basic needs of food, clothing, shelter, and safety and priority by providing case management or referring for services.
5. Consider using the creative arts in processing trauma.

The importance of secure caregiver child relationships cannot be underestimated in the ability of a child to heal from trauma. Perry & Hambrick (2008) said it best when they stated,

"Children with relational stability and multiple positive, healthy adults invested in their lives improve; children with multiple transitions, chaotic and unpredictable family relationships and relational poverty do not improve even when provided with the best "evidence-based' therapies" (p.43).

CHAPTER 6

Attention Deficit Hyperactivity Disorder

● ● ●

ACCORDING TO THE MOST RECENT CDC survey 11% of children aged 4-17 have ever been diagnosed with Attention Deficit Disorder, (ADHD). Currently the most common form of treatment is prescribed stimulant medication (Daley et al. 2014). Pelham et al. (2012) stated that this approach has limitations for several reasons including a tendency for many parents to prefer non-pharmacological approaches. In addition, they state that medication alone may be insufficient to enable the child/adolescent to function on a normal level and long term outcomes are not achieved. They advocate instead for a comprehensive summer treatment program using a variety of treatment methods based on social learning theory to accomplish individualized goals.

The second most popular method to managing ADHD is behavioral therapy which includes positive reinforcement to achieve manageable goals. Conclusions differ in the literature about the efficacy of behavioral approaches. One meta-analysis stated that behavior therapy is effective in treating ADHD (Fabian et at., 2009). Another meta-analysis qualified this considerably. It stated that it had no effect on core ADHD symptoms yet when ADHD was associated with conduct issues, behavioral interventions were helpful. They also helped in improving parenting, especially parents' sense of empowerment (Daley et al. 2014). The American Academy of Pediatrics (AAP) (2011) found that both behavioral therapy and medication was not significantly more effective than medication alone yet parents' satisfaction was higher with combined treatments.

The National Resource Center on ADHD which is a program of Children and Adults with ADHD (CHADD), a national organization which helps individuals and caregivers struggling with ADHD, states: "Behavioral interventions are also a major component of treatment for children who have ADHD." The Center's website goes on to describe strategies such as positive reinforcement, consistency, and problem solving. They also recommend that parents use a token or point system, plan ahead, take away privileges as consequences and use specific directions to manage their child's behavior and accomplish goals.

What do these differing conclusions mean for the PAH clinician? One of the most important principals is to collaborate with the caregiver. The AAP (2011) stated that in forming a treatment plan for a child with ADHD, family preference is essential. I have observed that some caregivers do not want to consider pharmacological treatment while others request it at the outset. Still others prefer behavioral treatments including parent training, skills building, and wish to try medication only as a "last resort." When collaborating, it is initially important to provide psychoeducation about the range of options parents have and current research regarding efficacy of treatment. Next, prioritizing concerns is key. For example, some children may have developed co-morbid issues either separate from or as a result of the ADHD. The caregiver may choose to focus on these first before dealing with typical ADHD symptomatology. 9-year-old Jess, for instance, started saying, "I'm nothing," to her mother. Her mother felt she was reacting to her chronically poor grades due to her lack of focusing and a recent falling out with a friend. The parent thought that working on building on self-esteem first would be more effective than tackling attention and impulsivity issues. Other parents and children may simply want to address the most challenging ADHD symptoms that are interfering with functioning such as getting ready for school without dawdling, completing a modified version of homework without 2 hours of fussing and distraction, or taking medicine in the AM without complaining and refusing for 40 min!

Another example of prioritizing concerns and working on them systematically is the case of Mindy whom you met in Chapter 2. The work with the therapist helped improve parenting and conduct at home and helped with some school behaviors yet her impulsivity and lack of focusing was not addressed adequately to maintain her in her present school. The parents chose at that point to seek a psychiatric consultation where she was given an ADHD diagnosis and stimulant medication. The parents changed her school to a more therapeutic setting. Due to scheduling conflicts with the new school which was farther away, outpatient therapy was terminated but reinstated about 6 months later. Mindy had done much better on medication and in the new school but continued to struggle with impulsivity in the home, school, and community. The parents found that they felt very supported and empowered when the therapist worked with them as a family to help them find solutions to the everyday interpersonal challenges presented by their child with ADHD.

TREATMENT

Once the PAH therapist has provided psychoeducation, prioritized concerns, and developed initial goals, treatment can begin. Frequently integrative approaches tend to work well to manage the variety of challenges that ADHD presents as well as the co-morbid conditions that may occur. For example, 6-year-old Oliver was defiant to authority figures and would deliberately break rules in school he did not wish to follow, e.g., coming in from recess, putting the ball away, assisting with clean up time, etc. He was also defiant at home, refusing to get ready for school, for instance, without a tantrum and seemed to "run the show," according to his parents. In addition, he had a tendency to lack the ability to sit in his seat in class and was highly distractible according to his teacher. Frequently he would get physical, e.g., "push" others when he felt they were in his space or if they slightly irritated him. Oliver was diagnosed with ADHD and ODD. Parents were not willing try pharmacological approaches at first but wanted to work on the ODD component with a parenting plan that could be coordinated with the school which the therapist could help to facilitate. Once parents felt they were more empowered they wanted to address other issues. During the course of treatment Oliver eventually benefitted from the following types of therapies, some of which are explained below and in the subsequent or prior chapters: parent management training, skills development (including problem solving and expressing feelings), relevant social skills training, psychiatric evaluation, school liaison, and reflective listening (parents).

Parenting plans

Behavioral plans to manage ADHD symptoms on the CHADD website recommend the same principles as most parenting programs such as the Nurtured Heart Approach or the Kazdin Method espouse. I have observed that these plans are highly effective yet I would add several strategies that address the ADHD child's distractibility that work well in the office setting and help parents get listened to at home. As a PAH therapist, I encourage the parent to incorporate these strategies when relevant into the parenting plan.

1. When addressing the child, say his/her name and request eye contact if the child is looking elsewhere. Once eye-contact is made, be brief and give the direction or ask the question. Stay to watch for follow through and repeat as children with ADHD may need repeated instructions. Having children also repeat back the direction can be helpful. One parent I know always tells her child that when the buzzer goes off, the TV will be turned off. She then quizzes her child, "What will happen when the buzzer goes off?" Unless her child repeats out loud to her what will happen, she will not turn it on. She also gives him 2 warnings a few minutes before the buzzer is about to go off. This exercise allows her ADHD child to fully process the information that this enjoyable activity will have an end. When she simply warns him without having him repeat out loud how the activity would end, he goes into a raging and sometimes destructive temper tantrum.

2. Children with ADHD have extra difficulty focusing on low interest activities. It is better for them to complete lower interest activities

first and then allow them the privilege to do higher interest activities. For example, parents who allow their ADHD child to do computer games after school for an hour to wind down find that it is nearly impossible for their child to then do their homework. It is better for their child to wind down without screen time, a high interest, highly stimulating activity, do their homework and other things they need to do and get rewarded with computer game time provided it is not too late.

3. Give directions with only as many steps as the child can successfully handle without getting distracted. For example, if Angie was told to get ready for school, she would procrastinate and get distracted yet if told, "Let's see how fast you can get dressed and come down to breakfast for pancakes," the prompt would be enough to organize her. Brian, on the other hand, would get totally lost in his Legos and fighting with his siblings if given Angie's directive. A more specific directive such as, "Put on the shirt that's on you bed and see if you can get your pants on before I come in and check on you," would be more effective for Brian. Lili, on the other hand, is so highly distractible, especially and among her large family that her mother has to stand by the door of her room if she wants Lili to get dressed independently. She needs to call out each step in the process of getting dressed. Lili's mother's script looks something like this: "Lili, take off your night gown. Good job! Now open your drawer. Can you find your underwear?... Great! Wow! you put it on very quickly. Here are your pants... Your shirt fell on the floor behind you. You can look at the doll shoe later. Just put on your shirt and you're almost done."

4. Framing requests or directions positively is mentioned in many parent training programs but I will re-emphasize it here. Children with ADHD need more directions because of their distractibility. Positivity is extra important simply because they hear more instruction. Examples of positivity are: "Can you please set the table?" "I'd like you to finish your homework before making that call." "Let's see how fast you can pick up your toys before the

guests arrive." There is no guarantee that positivity will insure compliance but as part of a total parenting package it may help make ADHD challenging behavior more manageable.

Play-Based Interventions
Skills Development Games

Children with ADHD have a range of challenges stemming from their impulsivity and difficulty focusing. Game play therapy where a therapeutic game is chosen to address a particular issue is one approach that works well when involving caregivers. In this instance, the therapist can be the game "coach" distributing tokens for answered questions or completing game activities and teaching and enforcing game rules while the parent and child(ren) play. The clinician can also follow up on an extra question or activity of his/her own if the game brings up a relevant issue that would be useful to expand upon. There are a few good published therapeutic skill building games that can be purchased through catalogue companies such as *Self-Esteem Shop* and *Childswork/Childsplay*. I will list a few of the most useful and fun games for children with ADHD and their families here. (Ordering information will be listed in the appendix). *Stop, Relax and Think* is good for introducing and practicing the concept of impulse control. *No More Arguments* teach children how to get out of arguing with others even if someone tries to start an argument first. *No More Bullies* deals with how to handle bullies but many of the cards challenge participants to think about "cool down" skills which are often essential to many children challenged by impulsive behavior. *Focus* is a new game I discovered that challenges a participant to do a task while being playfully distracted. The *Ungame* kids/teens version is a wonderful way to talk about kids and teens issues and helps with thinking and problem solving skills. There is also the entire set of coping skills balls that *Childswork/Childsplay* publishes which teaches anger and stress management, impulse control, self- esteem building, positive thinking skills, and more. These balls are handy to have inflated because, if a child is restless, there is usually a ball that is relevant to the goals of the program and the child and parent both enjoy a break from sitting.

GAMES TO FACILITATE EXPRESSION OF FEELINGS

Frequently an intervention plan for the ADHD child will include more opportunities to express feelings about everything. The hypothesis for these children is that they either hold feelings inside, need to develop the skill of self-expression or lack insight and that more opportunities and practice talking about feelings and experiences in a supportive setting with their caregiver's attention will reduce the tendency to act out feelings in a non-verbal disruptive way. There are a plethora of games published to facilitate expression of feelings. Some of my favorites include: *Exploring My World, Family Happenings Game, Bright Spots Cards, Ungame Cards,* and *Totika.* The therapist can also combine an activity the child enjoys with a feeling activity. For example, a child or adolescent who enjoys basketball can write ten to twenty different feelings on separate pieces of paper or this can be prepared separately by the therapist beforehand. The papers are shuffled and turned over and the client then picks out a piece of paper from the top. The client then reads aloud the word written and the therapist asks a question about the feeling that the client would be amenable to answering. For example, if the word was frustrated, the therapist might ask, "What is something in school that really frustrates students?" or if the word was happy, the therapist might ask, "What was the happiest time of your day today?" The client can refuse to answer any question but if he does answer, he gets to crush the paper into a ball and has three tries to make a "basket" into the office garbage can. The turn then passes to the parent. The client can be invited to ask their own question to the parent or the therapist can make one up.

ROLE PLAYS

Role plays can help the child practice new behaviors in a non-stressful setting. This can be helpful not only for the child with ADHD but also for any child whose goal is to achieve a new behavior such as reduced hitting, improved assertiveness, less bossy behavior, etc. I have observed that impulsive children frequently become reactive over the same or a similar stressor. The stressor does not change and if they lack the ability to slow down and problem solve for the next time, it happens over and over, getting them in constant trouble. I worked with an unmedicated boy with ADHD, Justin, who told me a girl kept calling him "Fuzzy Head" because of his hair cut. He is in a special class that heavily monitors his behavior. His teacher told him that he can advance to a higher level and obtain more privileges if he can contain himself and not disrupt the entire class should the girl bother him. When I asked him what he could do to improve his response to this teasing, he initially said he had no idea. An especially helpful role play for situations like the one described above is where the child not only practices more effective behaviors to handle an ongoing stressor that will likely not change but is challenged to repeat it many times so that he begins to get a bit more desensitized to the stressor. *For example, 8-year-old Adele's younger brother constantly teased her that she "likes Mr. Lake," the substitute gym teacher. Adele would get immediately riled up and become frequently aggressive which is likely what entertained her brother. The mother felt that her intervention efforts in this system were ineffective. In session, Adele was told that her brother was going to tease her like this again and again. She was given a choice of things to say back to him as a surprise, like, "Thank you," "Whatever," etc. She ended up choosing, "And your point is?" The role play was enacted where the mother played the part of the brother teasing Adele the exact way he does about how she "likes Mr. Lake." Adele said, "And your point is?" and walked away. The role play was repeated five times. The family was seen two weeks later and the report was that Adele had successfully managed to use the new behavior and was no longer reactive to that stressor. In fact, the mother commented that Adele managed to be even more patient than the parents themselves!* A similar type of desensitization role play was done with Justin where he planned to ignore the name calling. When he was seen the following week, he reported that the girl was no longer calling him names.

Anger Management Interventions

Sometimes caregivers notice that children with ADHD have difficulty with anger management and that expression of feelings, understanding, parent training, and other interventions are not enough to address the outbursts of anger that seem to be affecting the family. They and the children themselves often want anger management to be a goal. Anger management curriculums with a strong CBT component can work well for a child who needs these skills as a component of his treatment plan. (Sukhodolsky, Kassinove, & Gorman 2003; Ho, Carter, & Stephenson, 2010). The workbook, *What to do When Your Temper Flares*, by Dawn Huebner, PhD, is based on CBT approaches and can be introduced to the family. It provides a step by step explanation of how children can change their thoughts about external situations so that they can become less reactive. It also teaches children how to cool down so that they can more effectively problem solve. The therapist can introduce the curriculum by having the parent and child read a chapter of the work book together in the office and do one of the accompanying activities. The clinician can then supplement those activities and ideas with other multi-sensory activities. For example, *Childswork/Childsplay*, a therapeutic play catalogue, has a variety of activity and skill building balls, one of which is called the *Anger Control Ball*. The ball is thrown to family members and where their right thumbs land there is either a question regarding anger management such as, "What is one way to cool down when angry?" or an experiential exercise, "Count backwards from 10 slowly." Another supplementary activity is to help the child understand the mechanism of the brain and the role that stress plays in shutting down the frontal lobe as described in Chapter 4. Understanding why we get stressed and angry from a scientific perspective can help some children feel less "bad." At the same time, understanding why our brain needs time to "cool down" before tackling problem solving can provide greater motivation to work on calming down skills.

A special role play I like to do is to have the child play the part of the person who annoys him (which is frequently the sibling). I play the role of the child doing what the parent and I would wish the child would do instead of their usual maladaptive behavior if provoked. We frequently discover that if the child does what we wish, the situation would not be effectively managed. For example, we may enact a scenario where a child is encouraged to tell his mother about a problem with a baby brother touching a Lego model instead of beating him up. However, in the role play, the mother is busy nursing the newborn and would not be able to effectively intervene to prevent the model from being destroyed. This role play is very validating for the child and helps the parent and myself better understand the complexity of the child's situation. We can then come up with a plan that has a better chance of both solving the problem and avoiding aggression.

Reflective Listening

Sometimes it is simply difficult to be a child with ADHD and constantly challenged by having to work very hard to manage impulses and maintain focus. Children begin to realize that their siblings are given fewer directions, reprimands, and are generally in less trouble. They are aware they can be annoying to others but can feel misunderstood and alone even in the most supportive of family situations. In these cases, I recommend that the parent try reflective listening, a technique which can benefit all children but can be especially helpful when a child perceives he is misunderstood.

Reflective listening occurs when the parent or therapist simply reflects or "guesses" what a child is feeling without judgement even if they "disagree" that the child should feel that particular way. (Dinkmeyer & McKay, 1983) They continue to reflect until the child is fully validated. I coach parents that there are no "buts" in reflective listening, e.g., "I know you are angry at your brother but you can't hit him," as the child will only hear the admonishment and not the understanding of his feelings. I also coach parents that reflective listening does not involve problem solving and that immediate problem solving may minimize the effect of the validation. In addition it can be better to wait a bit because a child's feeling a sense of validation often changes his perspective of the issue. Reflective listening can be time consuming and one cannot process every incident or feeling in this way all the time but it can be effective if done periodically.

REFLECTIVE LISTENING CASE EXAMPLE

Corey, age 8 and oldest of 3 children, received medication for ADHD yet continued to have severe reactivity and aggression at home and mild focusing issues in school. The doctor was continuing to see what combination of medicines would address his symptoms yet so far the medical treatments had only been partially helpful. There is a history of ADHD in the family, yet parents are supportive, attentive and knowledgeable and had behavior modification systems in place that seem ineffective. As part of the overall treatment plan, the mother decided to use reflective listening as she noticed Corey seemed more irritable and despondent in the family. A typical interaction was as follows: Corey enjoys reading and his younger sister Fiona, sometimes looks over his shoulder to see what he is reading. His response is to yell at her and push her violently away. Fiona looks up to her big brother and cries to her mother because she is sometimes physically hurt but more often emotionally hurt by her brother's callous treatment of her which she has to endure frequently. Usually mother talks to Fiona about her feelings and admonishes or punishes Corey for 'using his hands." He loses the privilege to read in that location for a while. If the parent talks to Corey about his behavior, this is how the conversation typically goes:

Parent: Why did you push Fiona?
Corey: She was getting in my space as usual.
Parent: You could have just asked her to move and not pushed her.
Corey: I did ask her to move.
Parent: She said you just pushed her and I've seen you do things like this before.
Corey: OK Believe her, you always do.
Parent: Corey, even if you asked her first, you have to stop hurting people in the family. You have to come and tell me.
Corey: You never listen. You're always on their side.
Parent: That's because you've already hurt somebody!

Once the therapist coached the parent to do reflective listening either during a family session or as part of a parenting plan, the same conversation looked very different.

Parent: Why did you push Fiona?
Corey: She was bothering me and getting in my space as usual.
Parent: That really makes you mad.
Corey: I HATE that she always does that.
Parent: You can't stand that and it feels like she does it all the time.
Corey: Yes, I know she does it on purpose to annoy me.
Parent: So, you get even more mad because you think she does it on purpose.
Corey: She DOES it on purpose! Today she bobbed her head in and out from my book with a smile on her face.
Parent: That is so annoying.
Corey: Yeah and you never believe me! You are always on everyone else's side!
Parent: So you feel we're always on everyone else's side and against you.
Corey: Yes, you don't care. (Cries)
Parent: It has seemed to you all this time like we didn't care, (hugging him)

At this point the reflective listening has done it's work and the parent assured Corey she does care. She saw that Fiona had a bit more of a part to play in this than she saw previously but in any case, Corey had a chance to verbalize feelings and get validated. Note that the parent did not condone aggression in any way nor did she minimize Corey's concerns. Any behavioral or cognitive work done in the future will be easier if Corey knows his parents understand how sensitive he is to slight provocations and how hard it is for him to keep his cool.

Summary

Interventions with the child with ADHD are most successful if family preference is considered and integrative approaches are used. The literature does have conflicting accounts about the efficacy of behavioral approaches yet reports indicate that parents prefer them. Some of the behavioral approaches described in this chapter include positive reinforcement, and giving effective directions and prompts. Other techniques include game play therapy to increase skill building, and express feelings, role plays to practice new skills and problem solve and CBT techniques for anger management. The therapist will be most successful if these interventions are delivered in an upbeat and positive manner and have a variety of movement due to the energy of the children. For example: a role play followed by a board game and finishing with a ball activity can be especially successful because the movements are standing/sitting/standing and there is movement within each activity

CHAPTER 7

Social Skills

● ● ●

CHILDREN WHO HAVE SOCIAL SKILLS challenges as either a primary or secondary component of their presenting problem can benefit from social skills training. (Laugeson et. al., 2012; Ikporukpo, 2015; Cook et al., 2008; Boo & Prins, 2007). Frequently successful social skills training programs such as the UCLA PEERS program provide a combination of group skills training for the client, in this case the adolescent, with concurrent psychoeducational groups for the parents separately (Laugeson et.al, 2012). In a small agency or private practice setting, however, it may be difficult or nearly impossible to come up with a viable group of, for example, 6-8 similarly aged children available at the same time and day each week who request social skills help around the same time of the year. If there is an active group program it may not run in the summer months when they are requesting it or may not be accommodating their age category because there was not enough enrollment. In that case, a client either has to wait for the next cycle or is simply ineligible for that service.

A PAH approach can be an effective alternative to the traditional group training approach and can be an effective way to introduce social skills concepts to the child providing help right away in the event a group program is not readily available. In some instances, a PAH approach may even be preferable to a group approach because the goals and curriculum will be tailor made to the child's specific challenges and the parent can play a more dynamic role as observer and "social skills coach." As "coach," the parent can facilitate peer interactions that are commensurate with the child's ability and have the best chance of a child feeling successful. For example, a parent may help a painfully shy child plan an activity based play date by taking the child and classmate bowling. Since the focus will be on the activity as opposed to conversation and will be time limited, the child may be less anxious and have a more successful play date. An additional advantage in teaching social skills within a family setting is that frequently similar social issues that occur within the community occur in the family setting. For example, a child who tends to be bossy or a poor sport with classmates may show that same behavior with siblings or cousins. The family offers a "laboratory" with opportunities to practice new behaviors. Parents can identify the specific skill they would like their child to achieve, provide prompts to help them achieve it, and then provide either verbal praise or material rewards for the new behavior. *For example: Cindy, a 10-year-old girl with PDD had a problem with interrupting. She lacked both the impulse control to wait and recognize the social cues to know when it was acceptable to change the subject or make a request. She was told to say, "Excuse me," prior to interrupting yet this backfired because she would simply interrupt as before but say "Excuse me," before immediately going into her subject. In a family PAH session, she was given other ways to get acknowledged, e.g., standing next to the person and making eye contact or waiting until they finished their sentence before speaking, etc. Parents rewarded her with a dime in her piggy bank each time they "caught" her trying not to interrupt. In time, the interrupting was at a more manageable level and Cindy would just need occasional reminders.*

The therapist and family can work in conjunction with the school to hone in on particular skills. *For example, 6-year-old Abby who had a combination of reactivity issues as well as difficulty reading social cues attended an all-girl class. She would hit her classmates for lining up next to her even though they were instructed to do so to proceed to different activities. Because she liked a larger than usual degree of personal space, she lashed out at anyone who got too close and did not understand the degree of social ostracism and outrage she received from the other girls who did not attack her back, but instead, told their teacher what Abby just did. There was concern that Abby would be asked to leave the school. After talking with the teacher, the therapist drew a picture of Abby looking angry and with hands raised about to hit a child on line. She then drew a picture of Abby tolerating the person in front and behind her and not hitting. It was explained to*

Abby by the mother that she can no longer hit children that are lining up next to her because it is against school rules and she may have to be picked up from school or will not have recess if she does it again. The mother further explained that the children will begin to refuse to play with her because they do not want to be with someone who hits. Abby was shown the picture of how we want to help her go from the first picture of being the girl who hits to the second picture of being the girl who does not.

Abby was seen with her sister for this session and since her mother noticed that Abby frequently would frequently like to cuddle or would sometimes be physically overbearing with siblings she felt that Abby actually likes close physical proximity if she is in control. The therapist suggested that mother, Abby, and sister, Penny, play the "sandwich" game. In this game, someone plays the cheese and the two others play the "bread." They then stand until they are touching toe to toe and call out, "SANDWICH!" and then someone else gets to be the "cheese," who is the person who stands in the middle. The family played several rounds of this to help Abby become desensitized to the concept of space when lining up. Abby was then challenged to role play an actual school scenario where she had to line up and not hit another child even if she felt the child was too close. She was given a few tools to help her be successful such as deep breathing to relax her body and good thoughts such as, "If I don't hit, I will still have recess time!" Abby commented, "Anyway, I can pretend I am playing the sandwich game when I am lining up and it will be fun!" In a two week follow up the teacher reported that the hitting upon lining up was no longer an issue.

In addition to psychoeducation, role plays, family games, and behavior modification plans, PAH approaches can incorporate bibliotherapy as a starting off point for beginning a dialogue about social skills. Carol Gray, originator of the concept of *Social Stories* and who has published several books on the subject has provided simple stories to communicate social skills to children with social skills disabilities. Her newest book, published in 2015 is *The New Social Story Book* which has illustrations and 150 stories. A tool that I have recently begun successfully using with families are *Social Story Cards*. These are 6" photos of scenarios and on the back, is a social story. The cards are divided by category, school, family, and community. The names of the stories describe a social challenge, e.g., *I Can*

Wait to Speak Without Interrupting. Children are instructed to look at the picture while the instructor reads the back of the story. Whenever possible, I encourage the parent to read. The stories and pictures are designed for children from 5-12 on the autistic spectrum yet I have used them with much success with children who have social deficits stemming from the challenges of ADHD, mood dysregulation disorders, disruptive disorders, and reactivity or anger management difficulties. There are also a wealth of books published by Boys Town Press and frequently written by author, Julia Cook, addressing a range of social issues in a fun and engaging way such as *Teamwork Isn't My thing and I Don't Like to Share!* To find these books the therapist can make good use of visiting the children's section of the local library or take advantage of one of the best online book stores of children's therapeutic books which is the Self-Esteem Shop (www.selfesteemshop.com.) Introducing a social skills concepts through an illustrated story card or book read by the parent is an excellent non-stigmatizing way to start to address a social challenge. Board Games such as the *"You and Me"* game and *"No More Teasing"* are also fun ways of reinforcing and reviewing adaptive social skills concepts.

MULTIPLE FAMILY SOCIAL SKILLS GROUPS

There has been research which has shown that multiple family groups can be an effective intervention for children with disruptive behavior disorders such as OCD (Gopalan et al. 2015: McKay et. al., 1999). I have adapted the multiple family group format for social skills. Unlike the parallel group format where parents and children are divided, the multiple family social skills group (MFSSG) has parents and children together. The format that works best for the MFSSG, is to have 8 one hour long sessions. There are two or three sessions where parents and children are briefly divided for 10 or 15 minutes but for the bulk of the time, social skills are taught in a multi-sensory format in a variety of ways. I found that children with social skills issues are often cranky and tired after school when a group is most likely to be run so much of the learning is activity based and psychoeducation and discussion are participatory and short. Children learn about concepts through brief lecture done in an engaging format often with visual aids and skits. The learning is supplemented by large group activities and parent/child activities, role plays and discussion. An ideal group roster to start with is at least 8 families. There is frequently a drop of in enrollment due to unforeseen circumstances or absences due to illness so starting with a smaller number like 4 families may mean that some weeks only one family may show up which can greatly lower group morale and lead to the disbanding of the group. To have a good group dynamic it is best to have a minimum of 4 families present for each session.

A curriculum based on the needs and culture of the group participants is ideal and the most effective program will vary from group to group. However, once the therapist has developed activities and ideas that have worked for a particular topic, they can be reused for the next group if it seems that the same topic should again be presented. Parents can fill out a brief questionnaire or simply be interviewed by telephone to help guide the therapist as to the social skills challenges of the participants and what issues should be addressed. Unlike family work, not all issues presented in the MFSSG will directly address each child's particular struggle. For example, in a group sample only three participants may need skills regarding respect for authority, two may need help in conversation skills, four need ideas on how to handle teasing and only one needs to learn how to interact without being a bully. The therapist may decide that there is value on focusing on each of these topics both for the benefit of the child who is struggling and for the indirect benefit it can have for children with other issues. Conversation skills for example may help the bully learn to interact appropriately and help victims of teasing practice assertiveness indirectly.

There are usually 5-8 activities within each session and parents are given "homework" for each week to help their children practice a skill. The homework might simply be to notice and praise when they observe their child working on a skill learned in the group or could get more involved such as scheduling a play date and observing strengths and challenges. Topics that I have found to be generally of interest to parents include making and keeping friends, respect for authority, handling teasing, impulse control, self-esteem, recognizing social cues, and bullying others.

A typical multiple family group session format would include the following activities;

1. Short participatory large group discussions or presentations on topics. Presentations may include skits, video clips, or stories augmented by visual aids.
2. Large group activities which demonstrates concepts such as children/parents reading a skit or enacting a role play, doing a brainstorming activity, skill building ball game, etc.
3. Parent/child activity. Parents and children are given a task such as a board game, interactional activity, art project, or creative activity to practice the skill presented while the leaders move around the room to coach parents and children.

    A sample outline from our MFSSG curriculum on Conversation Skills is as follows:

1. Group Discussion: How do we make a friend? What do we say? (Leaders will focus on the skills of saying, "Hi," and introducing oneself and asking a question. This can be followed up by asking another question or saying something relevant.)
2. Skit with Leaders and Children:
    Skit #1: 2 participants are instructed to play "catch" with a rubber ball. The leader comes near the children and says, "Hi," in a low voice while the participants are instructed to ignore her. The leader walks away. End of skit.

    Group Discussion: The leader asks, "Did I do anything wrong?"

    (The hoped-for answer is that the children will recognize that the leader did indeed say "Hi" but did not say it in a loud enough voice and did not ask a question like, "Can I play?")

    Another child is asked to "redo" the skit, taking the role of the leader and doing it the "right" way.

3. Skit #2: Child participant and leader. Below is the skit script given to leader and child:

    Leader: Hi Sam

    Child: Hi

    Leader: What did you think of that test?

    Child: It was really hard. I don't think I did well.

    Leader: Are you kidding? It was SO EASY! I'm sure I got a 100%. Today I am having spaghetti.

    (Child walks away.) End of skit.

    Leader asks, "Did I do anything wrong?"

    (The hoped-for response is that the leader did say, "Hi," and asked a question but the follow up comment was rude and hurtful and the spaghetti comment was way off topic. The group can then discuss what would be a better response.)

4. The parents and children are instructed to play a game with each other to reinforce this concept. Parents are given 12 chips each. Children are given a list of three questions to ask their parents which include:

    a. How was your day today?

    b. What is one of your favorite things to do?

    c. What do you like your family to do to help you?

    The child gets one chip for good eye contact, (a concept previously learned in another session), another chip if he can remember and repeat the parent's answer and 2 chips if he can ask a follow up question or say something related to the parent's answer. The child wins if he can earn at least 8 chips. Group leaders go around to the individual families playing the games to help with any interpersonal problems which may arise, e.g., child refuses to play, a parent needs help in using prompts in order to help his child succeed, both parent and child need encouragement, etc. (Parents often comment that they love this game as their children never ask them how THEY feel and they are delighted to be asked and listened to.)

5. Ball Game: As a group, the *You and Me* Ball Game to reinforce positive social skills is played. This will provide some movement for the group.

6. Depending on the group's energy and ability to focus, a new topic could be introduced as the activities described above will take about 35 minutes provided the group starts on time. Leaders could also review skills learned in a previous group and have participants make a poster with markers and stickers. Some group leaders like to take this time to teach mindfulness and children and parents are given 2-minute meditation focusing on the feel and texture of Play-Doh. (See Chapter 4) Because many of the children we see for social skills also have impulsivity and reactivity, this is a useful skill to introduce. Children and parents can continue to play with the Play-Doh while the therapists discuss and distribute the parent's "homework." For this week it would be to notice and praise the child for doing any of the skills discussed in this session and to observe the child interacting with peers and taking careful note of current strengths and challenges.

Summary

Social skills training can be accomplished with a PAH approach and can be an excellent alternative if a group program is not available. It can supplement a group program that does not have a strong parent training component or does not focus on the particular skills the child needs help with. The therapist can encourage the parent to take on the role of "social skills coach" and provide positive opportunities for the child to practice new skills within the family setting. A MFSSG is another excellent alternative to introduce the child to social skills concepts, practice new behaviors, and begin a dialog about positive social interaction between parent and child.

CHAPTER 8

When Things Are Not Working

● ● ●

NEIGHBORS OF MINE RECENTLY TOLD me that their son had such a fear of balloons that one could not mention the word, "balloon" without his becoming visibly anxious, e.g., worried expression, clingy behavior, and shortness of breath. If he suspected a balloon was in the vicinity, he would refuse to go forward and if he actually saw a balloon he would shriek and run away in a panic. The parents took him for individual therapy for years, hoping the therapy would improve his fears. When they asked what they could do to help, the therapist gave them little direction. Despite the fact that his phobic reaction toward balloons did not change, they continued to take him because it was "recommended." Eventually when the parents felt the treatment was having no effect on their son's condition they withdrew him from treatment. Years later their son lost his fear of balloons as he entered adolescence.

A scenario such as the one described above is not likely to happen using a PAH approach because the PAH therapist would be continually evaluating the effectiveness of his work in partnership with the parent. Because the therapist is in close contact with the family and frequently the school and community system, he has the opportunity for more feedback from multiple sources. However, it has been my experience and observation that one can have the "best" assessment and plan yet it still does not address the problems in a significant enough way to make an impact. Other times a plan that has been working well suddenly stops working and the child or adolescent regresses.

There are many reasons why a plan may not be working and I will list a few of the more common ones here:

1. The original hypothesis, "why" the child/adolescent is having symptoms, may be wrong.
2. The goals need to be scaled back, e.g., instead of behavioral compliance on multiple levels the child may be initially only be able to accomplish reduced physical aggression.
3. The intervention plan needs better follow through at home.
4. A stressor regarding the child's emotional state was added, e.g., change to a new school, change in visitation schedule with the biological parent, peer pressure, etc.
5. The family or child needs more services in order for the child to get significantly better, e.g., case management, psychiatric services, marital therapy, remedial education, hospitalization, child protective services, etc. may need to be added.
6. The hypotheses may be "right" yet the child is not responsive to the intervention so thinking "outside the box" and trying something new may be successful.

If this should happen the therapist can sit down with the caregivers and if appropriate the child/adolescent to evaluate what might be missing and brainstorm ways to make the treatment more effective. Below are examples of cases where a child either did not make progress or regressed and how the therapist in conjunction with the family addressed the situation.

Case Vignettes
David

David, whom you met in the introduction was still in therapy when his mother, Sarah, commented that he continued to have huge meltdowns whenever he was told, "No," he could not do or have something he wanted. Sarah was to add reflective listening we called "Super Empathy," when David was told, "No." We observed it took the edge off of David's reactivity. When we reviewed Sarah's home strategy for dealing with David, she acknowledged that she had initially been doing the "Super Empathy" which had been helpful but had not done it at all in a long time and had not even realized it. We decided to reinstate it to see if it would have any effect. The next time the family was seen Sarah reported that she began using it and David was much calmer and better able to hear a "no" answer.

JOEY

6-year-old Joey seemed an outwardly happy child yet at home continued to have defiance and toileting accidents. Many hypotheses were formed and interventions tried but it seemed Joey was not getting significantly better. The therapist had wanted to do some home visits for a fuller assessment but the family refused this service. Finally, because the family's car needed to be in the repair shop for an extended period, the family agreed to have the therapist do home visiting for a month. During this time, the therapist observed that the mother and father were loving yet very distracted by a variety of things including their toddler twins. Joey's older brother Jimmy who had severe impulsivity issues was a bully to Joey. Joey would respond by acquiescing to Jimmy's demands or crying. Because Joey had more of a low-key way of responding to Jimmy, the distracted family did not see it as much of an issue. When the therapist saw this happening several times in the home she intervened to stop it and informed the parents. The following week the mother said that Joey's toileting and behavior was better and he concurrently started talking about his frustration about Jimmy to the therapist. It was felt that previous treatments were not effective because the impact of Jimmy's bullying on Joey was not considered.

CLARE

Clare, a 12-year-old who was living with her grandparents had a history of physical and sexual abuse and neglect. While she was somewhat stable for the past two years, it started becoming difficult to get family involvement and in time, the family would rarely return phone calls. Often a friend of the family would drop Clare off for appointments. The therapist found that with the onset of adolescence, Clare began abusing her prescribed psychiatric medication, smoking marijuana and having unprotected sex. She urged the caregivers to explore other treatment options such as a drug and alcohol program, family planning clinic, or a dual diagnosis facility. Eventually the caregivers realized outpatient therapy did not adequately address Clare's needs and Clare fortunately was eligible for higher levels of services, eventually getting some stability at a residential treatment facility. In a few years, she was able to resume outpatient work.

Summary

Frequently in the course of treating a child or adolescent there may be a need to reassess if goals are not being achieved in a timely way. The PAH approach provides constant access to the caregivers who are partners with the therapist in healing. This team approach enables the client to readily access the most effective treatment for their issues.

The PAH approach recognizes the power of the caregiver to heal their child with therapeutic support and a sound intervention. Clinicians new to this method can be off to a good start by simply communicating their appreciation of caregiver input and a willingness to collaborate. It is hoped that the PAH approach will be useful for the readers' "toolkit" in their work with children and adolescents and that it will lead to great fun, creativity, and a dynamic therapeutic partnership!

• • •

Good websites to order materials:

1. www.selfesteemshop.com has a wealth of books for bibliotherapy as well as play therapy toys and games. The owner, Deanne, reads all of her inventory and can direct you to any subject you are interested in. The phone number is 800-251-8336.
2. www.childswork.com also carries a great deal of therapeutic games and activities and a variety of feelings posters.
3. www.creativetherapystore.com is a smaller store yet it carries some items that the other stores do not carry.

Games/Activities to Promote Expression of Feelings and/or Family Communication

Bright Spots Cards Games by Elizabeth Wornham, LCSW, RPT-S, *Imago* [9]

Ungame Board Game with All Ages, Families, Kids, or Teens Cards, *Talicor*

Family Happenings Game, *Kids in Progress*

Exploring My World by Arley Loeffler, LCSW, *Western Psychological Services*

---

9 Where available, the developer or author is listed. The publisher is listed in italics at the end.

Laminated Feelings Posters, *various publishers*
Feelings Color Cards, *Speechmark*
Talk it Over Families Version, *Childswork/Childsplay*

GAMES/ACTIVITIES TO PROMOTE SELF-ESTEEM
Totika- Self Esteem Game by Scott Seiura, MS, *Open Spaces*
I Am Proud Ball, *Wellness Reproductions*

GAMES/ACTIVITIES TO PROMOTE IMPULSE CONTROL, ANGER MANAGEMENT, AND/OR FOCUSING
Stop, Relax, and Think Board Game by Becky Bridges, CSW, ACPA, *Childswork/Childsplay*
Stop Relax and Think Ball, *Childswork/Childsplay*
Focus Card Game, *Franklin Learning Systems*
Anger Strategies Ball, *Wellness Reproductions*
What to Do When Your Temper Flares, by Dawn Huebner, PhD, a workbook on anger management for parent and child to do together based on CBT skills published by *Magination Press.*

GAMES/ACTIVITIES TO PROMOTE SOCIAL SKILLS
You & Me Social Skills Board Game, *Childswork/Childsplay*
You & Me Counseling Ball, *Childswork/Childsplay*
Photo Social Stories Cards by Lawrence E. Shapiro, PhD. & Mike Canavan, *Childswork/Childsplay*
The New Social Story Book by Carol Gray, *Future Horizons*
The Helping, Sharing, and Caring Ball, *Childswork/Childsplay*
No More Bullies, *Childswork/Childsplay*
No More Arguments, *Childswork/Childsplay*

GAMES/ACTIVITIES TO PROMOTE ANXIETY REDUCTION

What to Do When You Worry Too Much by Dawn Huebner, PhD, workbook based on CBT skills for parent and child to do together published by *Magination Press.*

Less Stress Ball, *Childswork/Childsplay*

Exploring My World by Arley Loeffler, LCSW, *Childswork/Childsplay*

BIBLIOGRAPHY

About ADHD (2015). National Resource Center on ADHD, A Program of CHADD. Retrieved March 10, 2017, from http://www.help4adhd.org

Ahmann, E. & Dokken, D. (2014) Encouraging positive behavior in challenging children : the nurtured heart approach. *Pediatric Nursing*, 40 (1), 38-42.

Anrnsten, A, Mazure, C., Sinha, R. (2012, April) This is your brain in meltdown. Scientific American, 306(4), 48-53.

Adam, B.L., McGuire, J.F., Murphy, T.K. & Storch, E.A. (2014) The importance of considering parent's preferences when planning treatment for their children-the case of childhood obsessive-compulsive disorder. *Journal of Child Psychology and Psychiatry*, 55(12), 1314-1316.

Albano, A.M. & Kendall, P.C. (2002) Cognitive behavioural therapy for children and adolescents with anxiety disorders : clinical research advances. *International Review of Psychiatry*, 14, 129-134.

American Academy of Pediatrics (2011) ADHD : Clinical practice guideline for the diagnosis, evaluation, and treatment of attention-deficit/hyperactivity disorder in children and adolescents. *Pediatrics*, 128, 5, 1-16

APA Presidential Task Force on Evidence-Based Practice (2006). Evidence-based practice in psychology. *American Psychologist*, 6(4), 271-285.

Baggerly, J, Green, E, & Myrick, A. (2015) *Counseling Families.* Lanham : Rowman and Littlefield

Boo, G.& Prins, P. (2007) Social incompetence in children with ADHD: Possible moderators and mediators in social-skills training. *Clinical Psychology Review.* 27(1), 78-97.

Booth, P.B. & Jernberg, A.M. (2010). *Theraplay: Helping parents and children build better relationships through attachment based-play* (Third edition). San Francisco, CA: Jossey-Bass.

Bourne, E.J. (2010) *The anxiety and phobia workbook.* Oakland: New Harbinger Publications.

Bratton, S.C., Ray, D., & Jones, L (2005). The efficacy of play therapy with children: A meta- analytic review of treatment outcomes. *Professional Psychology: Research and Practice*, 36, 376-390.

Brennan, A. L., Hektner, J.L., Brotherson, S.E., & Harisen, T. M. (2016). A non-randomized evaluation of a brief nurtured heart approach parent training program. *Child and Youth Care Forum*, 45(5), 709-715.

Cappadocia, C. & Weiss, J. (2011) Review of social skills training groups for youth with Asperger syndrome and high functioning autism. *Research in Autism Spectrum Disorders.* 5(1), 70-78.

Carr, A. (2014) The evidence base for family therapy and systemic interventions for child *focused problems. Journal of Family Therapy, 36(2), 107-157.*

Caspe, M. Seltzer, A., Kennedy, J.L., Cappio, M. & DeLorenzo, C.(2013) Engaging families in the child assessment process. *National Association for the Education of Young Children* (Pamphlet) New York.

Cavett, Angela M, (2012). Structured play-based intervention for engaging children and adolescents in therapy: Infinity.

Cornett, N., & Bratton, S. (2015). A golden intervention: 50 years of research on filial therapy. *International Journal of Play Therapy*, 24(3), 119-133.

Cook, C., Gresham, F. Kern, L. Berreras, R., Thornton, S., Crews, S. (2008). Social skills training for secondary students with emotional and/or behavioral disorders, a review and analysis of the meta-analytic literature. *Journal of Emotional and Behavioral Disorders.* 16(3), 131-141.

Crane, D.R. & Christenson, J.D. (2012) A summary report of the cost-effectiveness of the profession and practice of marriage and family therapy. *Contemporary Family Therapy, 34, 204-216.*

Crenshaw, D. (2006) Neuroscience and trauma treatment: implications for creative arts therapists. In L. Carey (Ed.) *Expressive and creative arts methods for trauma survivors* (pp.21-38).

Daley, D., van der Oord, S., Ferrin, M., Danckaerts, M. Doepfner, M. Cortese, S. et al. (2014) Behavioral interventions in attention-deficit hyperactivity disorder: a meta-analysis of randomized controlled trials across multiple outcome domains. *Journal of the American Academy of Child & Adolescent Psychiatry, 53(8) 835-855.*

Dinkmeyer, D & McKay G. (1983) *The Parent's Guide STEP/TEEN.* Circle Pines, MN.: American Guidance Service.

Dretzke, J. Davenport, c. Frew, e. Barlow, J. Stewart-Brown, S. Baylis, S. (2009) The clinical effectiveness of different parenting programmes for children with conduct problems: a systematic review of random-ized controlled trials. *Child and Adolescent Psychiatry and Mental Health,* 3 (1), 7-19.

Eyberg, S.M., O'Brien, K.A., &Chase, R.M. (2006). Oppositional defi-ant disorder and parent training. In J.E. Fisher & W. T. O'Donohue (Eds.), *Practitioner's guide to evidence-based psychotherapy.* New York: Springer.

Fabiano, G.A., Pelham, W.E., Coles, E.K., Gnagy, E. M., Chronis-Tuscano, A & O0Connor, B.C. (2009) A meta-analysis of behavioral treatments for attention-deficit/hyperactivity disorder. *Clinical Psychology Review*, 29 (2), 129-140

Forgatch, M.S. & Patterson, G.R. (2012) Parent Management Training---Oregon Model. In Weicz, J.R. & Kazdin, A.E., (Eds.) Evidence-Based Psychotherapies for Children and Adolescents (pp.159-178). New York: Guilford.

Gil, E. (2015). *Play in family therapy (Second edition)*. New York, NY: Division of Guilford Publications, Inc.

Glasser, H & Easley, J. (1998) *Transforming the difficult child, the nurtured heart approach. Tucson, AZ: Howard Glasser.*

Goldfinch, M. (2009) Putting humpty together again: working with parents to help children who have experienced early trauma. *The Australian and New Zealand Journal of Family Therapy, 30 (4), 284-299.*

Gopalan, G., Chacko, A., Franco, L. Dean-Assail, K. Rotka, L, Marcus, S., Hoagwood, K., McKay, M. (2015) Multiple family groups for children with disruptive behavior disorders: child outcomes at 6-month follow-up. *Journal of Child and Family Studies. 24, 2721-2733*

Graves, K. & Shelton, T. (2009). Utilization of Individual versus family therapy among adolescents with severe emotional disturbance. *American Journal of Family therapy, 37, 227-238.*

Green, E.J. & Myrick, A.C. (2014) Treating complex trauma in adolescents: a phase-based, integrative approach for play therapists. *International Journal of Play Therapy.* 23(3), 131-145.Guerney, L. (2000) Filial therapy into the 21st century. *International Journal of Play Therapy, (9)2, 1-17.*

Guerney, B. (1964) Filial therapy: description and rationale. *Journal of Consulting Psychology.* 28(4), 304-310.

Guo K. & Slesnick, N. (2013) Family versus individual therapy: impact on discrepancies between parents' and adolescents' perceptions over time. *Journal of Marital & Family Therapy, 39(2) 182-194.*

Hektner, J.M, Brennan, A.L., Brotherson, S.E., (2013) A review of the nurtured heart approach to parenting: evaluation of its theorectical and empirical foundations. *Family Process, 52* (3), 425-439.

Heneggler, S., Sheidow, A. (2012). Empirically supported family-based treatments for conduct disorder and delinquency in adolescents. *Journal of Marriage and Family Therapy, 38*(1), 30-58.

Ho, Betty, Carter, Mark & Stephenson, J. (2010) Anger management using a cognitive-behavioral approach for children with special education needs: a literature review and meta-analysis. *International Journal of Disability, Development, and Education, 57(3), 245-261.*

Ikporukpo, A. (2015) Enhancing friendship-making ability of peer rejected adolescents through social skills training. *Ife PsychologIA*, 23(1), 157-167.

Ivanova, M.Y. et. al. (2007) Testing the 8-syndrome structure of the child behavior checklist in 30 societies. *Journal of Clinical Child and Adolescent Psychology, 36(3), 405-417.*

Kazdin, A. E. (2012) Problem-solving skills training and parent management training for oppositional defiant disorder and conduct disorder. In Weicz, J.R. & Kazdin, A.E., (Eds.), *Evidence-Based Psychotherapies for Children and Adolescents* (pp.211-226). New York: Guilford.

Kazdin, A.E. (2008) Evidence-based treatment and practice. *American Psychologist, 6(3), 146-159.*

Kazdin, A.E. (2005). *Parent management training.* New York, NY: Oxford University Press, Inc.

Kazdin, A.E. & Wassel, G. (2000). Therapeutic changes in children, parents, and families resulting treatment of children with conduct problems. *Journal of the American Academy of Child and Adolescent Psychiatry,* 39(4), 414-420.

Kazdin, A.E. & Weisz, J. (1998) Identifying and developing empirically supported child and adolescent treatments. *Journal of Consulting and Clinical Psychology, 66*(1) 19-36.

Kendall, P.C., Furr, J.M. & Podell, J.L. (2012) Child-focused treatment of anxiety. In Weicz, J.R. & Kazdin, A.E. (Eds.), *Evidence-Based Psychotherapies for Children and Adolescents* (pp 45-61). New York: Guilford.

Linehan, M.M. (1993) *Skills training manual for treating borderline personality disorder.* New York: Guilford Press.

Lowenstein, Liana (2010). *Creative family therapy techniques.* Toronto, Champion Press.

Laugeson, E., Frankel, F. Gantman, A. Dillon, A. &Mogil, C.(2012) Evidence-based social skills training for adolescents with autism spectrum disorders: the UCLA PEERS program. *Journal of Autism and Developmental Disorders, 42*(6), 1025-1042.

Mackinnon, L. (2012). The neurosequential model of therapeutics: An interview with Bruce Perry. *Australian and New Zealand Journal of Family Therapy, 33*(2), 210-218.

McLean, C., Asnaani, A. & Foa, E. (2015). Prolonged Exposure Therapy. In Schnyder, U. & Cloitre, M. (Eds.) *Evidence based treatment for trauma-related psychological disorders: a practical guide for clinicians.* (pp. 143-159). Switzerland: Springer International Publishing.

McKay, M., Gonzales, J Quintana, E. Kim, L., Abdul-Adil, J. (1999) Multiple family groups: an alternative for reducing disruptive behavioral difficulties of urban children. *Research on Social Work Practice. 9(5), 593-607.*

Munns, E & Munns, C (2015) Including families in Theraplay with children. In E. Green, A. Myrick, & J. Baggerly (Eds.), *Counseling Families (pp. 21-34).* Lanham: Rowman & Littlefield.

Munns, E. (2009). *Applications of family and group Theraplay.* Lanham: Jason Aronson.

Norton, A.R., Abbott, M. Norberg, M.M. & Hunt, C. (2015) A systematic review of mindfulness and acceptance-based treatments for social anxiety disorder. *Journal of Clinical Psychology, 71(4), 283-301.*

Perry, B. (2009) Examining child maltreatment through a neurodevelopmental lens: Clinical applications of the neurosequential model of therapeutics. *Journal of Loss and Trauma,* 14, 240-255.

Perry, B. & Hambrick, E. (2008). The neurosequential model of therapeutics. *Reclaiming Children and Youth,* 17, 3.

Perry, B & Szalavitz, M. (2006). *The boy who was raised as a dog.* Philadelphia, PA: Basic Books.

Prather, W. & Golden, J (2009) A behavioral perspective of childhood trauma and attachment issues: toward alternative treatment approaches for children with a history of abuse. *International Journal of Behavioral Consultation and Therapy,* 5(2), 222-241.

Read, K, Puleo, C., Wei, C. Cummings, C. Kendall, P. (2013) Cognitive-behavioral treatment for pediatric anxiety disorders. In R.A. Vasa and A.K. Roy (Eds). Pediatric anxiety disorders: a clinical guide, current clinical psychiatry (pp. 269-287). New York: Springer Science & Business.

Robin, A.L., Siegel, P.T. Moye, A.W. Gilroy, M., Dennis A.B., & Sikand, A. (1999) A controlled comparison for family versus individual therapy for adolescents with anorexia nervosa. *Journal of the American Academy of Child and Adolescent Psychiatry, 38(12) 1482-1489.*

Rubin, J. (2006) Foreword. In L. Carey (Ed.) *Expressive and creative arts methods for trauma survivors* (p. 10).

Semple, R.J., Lee, J., Rosa, D. & Miller L. F. (2010) A randomized trial of mindfulness-based cognitive therapy for children: promoting mindful attention to enhance social-emotional resiliency in children. *Journal of Child and Family Studies*, 19, 218-229.

Semple, R.J., Reid, E.F., & Miller, L. Treating anxiety with mindfulness: an open trial of mindfulness training for anxious children. *Journal of Cognitive Psychotherapy: An International Quarterly, 19(4), 379-392.*

Sori, C.F & Sheryl S. (2014) Integrating a neurosequential approach in the treatment of traumatized children: an interview with Eliana Gil, part II. *The Family Journal: Counseling and Therapy for Couples and Families, 22(2) 251-257.*

Sprenkle, D.H. (2012) Intervention research in couple and family therapy: a methodological and substantive review and introduction to the special issue. *Journal of Marital and Family Therapy, 38 (1), 3-29.*

Sukhodolsky, D., Kassinove, H., & Gorman, B. (2004) Cognitive-behavioral therapy in children and adolescents: a meta-analysis. *Journal of Aggression and Violent Behavior,* 9, 247-269.

Swift, J.K. & Callahan, J.L. (2009) The impact of client treatment preferences on outcome: a meta-analysis. *Journal of clinical Psychology,* 65(4) 368-381.

Tompkins, K.A., Swift, J.K. & Callahan, J.L. (2013) Working with clients by incorporating their preferences. *Psychology,* 50(3), 279-283.

Tercelan, A.E., Zamora, M.M., Moraga, J.M. & Garcia, A.J. The effectiveness of relaxation techniques in anxiety disorders. *European Psychiatry, 30, 1112.*

Urquiza, A.J. & Blacker, D. (2011) Parent-child interaction therapy for sexually abused children. In P. Goodyear-Brown (Ed.), *Handbook of Child Sexual Abuse: Identification, Assessment, and Treatment* (pp279-293). Hoboken: Wiley.

Urquiza, A.J. & Blacker, D. (2012) Parent-child interaction therapy: enhancing parent-child relationships. *Psychosocial Intervention, 21(2), 145-156.*

VanFleet, R (2014) *Filial therapy: Strengthening parent-child relationships through play. (Third Edition).* Sarasota, FL: Professional Resource Press.

Van der Kolk, B. A. (2005) Developmental trauma disorder. *Psychiatric Annals, 35(5), 401-408.*

Van Westrhenen, N. & Fritz, E. (2014) Creative arts therapy as treatment for child trauma: an overview. *The Arts in Psychotherapy, 41, 527-534.*

Weir, K., Lee, S. Canosa, P. Rogrigues, N. McWilliams, M. & Parker, L.,(2013) Whole family Theraplay: integrating family systems theory and Theraplay to treat adoptive families. *Adoption Quarterly, 16, 175-200.*

Zeqaj, F. (2015). The influence of integrative play therapy on children. *Academic Journal of Business Administration, Law and Social Sciences. 1*(3) 188-192.